WHEN THE BRIDE IS ATTACKED

KIRK E. FARNSWORTH, PHD

When the Bride Is Attacked by Kirk Farnsworth
Published by Creation House
A Strang Company
600 Rinehart Road
Lake Mary, Florida 32746
www.strangbookgroup.com

This book or parts thereof may not be reproduced in any form, stored in a retrieval system, or transmitted in any form by any means—electronic, mechanical, photocopy, recording, or otherwise—without prior written permission of the publisher, except as provided by United States of America copyright law.

Unless otherwise noted, scripture quotations are from the Holy Bible, New International Version. Copyright © 1973, 1978, 1984, International Bible Society. Used by permission.

Scripture quotations marked Berkeley are from *The Berkeley Bible* (Grand Rapids, MI: Zondervan, 1959).

Scripture quotations marked TLB are from The Living Bible. Copyright © 1971. Used by permission of Tyndale House Publishers, Inc., Wheaton, IL 60189. All rights reserved.

Scripture quotations marked NLT are from the Holy Bible, New Living Translation, copyright © 1996. Used by permission of Tyndale House Publishers, Inc., Wheaton, IL 60189. All rights reserved.

Scripture quotations marked AMP are from the Amplified Bible. Old Testament copyright © 1965, 1987 by the Zondervan Corporation. The Amplified New Testament copyright © 1954, 1958, 1987 by the Lockman Foundation. Used by permission.

Scripture quotations marked The Message are from *The Message: The Bible in Contemporary English,* copyright © 1993, 1994, 1995, 1996, 2000, 2001, 2002. Used by permission of NavPress Publishing Group.

Scripture quotations marked KJV are from the King James Version of the Bible.

Scripture quotations marked NAS are from the New American Standard Bible. Copyright © 1960, 1962, 1963, 1968, 1971, 1972, 1973, 1975, 1977 by the Lockman Foundation. Used by permission. (www.Lockman.org)

Scripture quotations marked RSV are from the Revised Standard Version of the Bible. Copyright © 1946, 1952, 1971 by the Division of Christian Education of the National Council of the Churches of Christ in the USA. Used by permission.

Excerpts from *Sheep in Wolves' Clothing: How Unseen Need Destroys Friendship and Community and What to Do About It* by Valerie J. McIntyre (Grand Rapids, MI: Baker Books, a divison of Baker Publishing Group, 1999) used by permission.

Cover design by Nathan Morgan

Copyright © 2010 by Kirk Farnsworth
All rights reserved

Library of Congress Control Number: 2010937176
International Standard Book Number: 978-1-61638-256-8

First Edition

10 11 12 13 14 — 9 8 7 6 5 4 3 2 1
Printed in the United States of America

To

THE KING'S GATHERING

Stepping over the threshold and joining the great harvest

Providing facilities for community-based service groups that are suitable for their activities and utilizing interactive relationships—between their members and church members participating in their activities—for starting spiritual conversations

Putting the kingdom first and making disciples who make disciples

And to

Family members and friends of the church in far away places who have prayerfully stood with us through good times and bad times, as Jesus continues to build His faithful little church

The real tragedy is that as church we have come to respect "acceptance" of intolerable situations, to "live with" a situation not knowing where to turn next.
— John Howard Yoder

Live for righteousness—it is God's will that your good lives should silence those who make foolish accusations against you.
—1 Peter 2:24, 15, NLT

God's order is the order of peace, but it is always based upon purity, for the wisdom that is from above is first pure and then peaceable.
— G. Campbell Morgan

Holiness is the mark of Thy house.
—Psalm 93:5, Berkeley

Whoever would love life and see good days must keep his tongue from evil and his lips from deceitful speech. He must turn from evil and do good; he must seek peace and pursue it. For the eyes of the Lord are on the righteous and his ears are attentive to their prayer, but the face of the Lord is against those who do evil.
—1 Peter 3:10–12

Contents

Introduction 1

Part I: Reality

1 Reviewing Underlying Issues 13

2 Revealing Psychological Dynamics 27

3 Recognizing Spiritual Warfare 41

4 Restoring Church Purity 59

Part II: Choice

5 Resolving the Conflict 75

6 Recovering from Conflict 93

7 Reframing the Future 111

8 Returning to Your First Love 125

| 9 | Reflecting on Loose Ends | 143 |

Appendix I: Acknowledging Transference 153

Appendix II: Acknowledging Self-Deception 155

Notes 157

About the Author 166

Introduction

Conflict is inevitable. Just like taxes and death. We also know it isn't always necessary, and it isn't fun. Everyone knows that, so why do we act like it is necessary for getting something done, and why do we actually enjoy having a good fight? Conflict stirs our emotions, focuses our thoughts, and clarifies our relationships and more. We hate it, and we love it. We flee from it, and we feed it.

Conflict and crazy go together. The dictionary defines *crazy* as unsound, flawed, shaky, unbalanced, and even insane. It also defines *crazy* as enthusiastic or eager, as in "I'm crazy about you" or being caught up in the excitement of periodic conspiracies. People fear conflict, and they enjoy conflict!

Consequently, I am putting conflict and crazy together in this book about the insane circumstances in church conflict. Crazy circumstances are almost always present and usually determine how conflicts are defined in the church. The craziness that actually causes church conflicts is potentially equally divided among the people, the leadership, and the church organization. All three can play a key role in creating crazy circumstances in church conflict. My focus in this book is on the people in the church. Warren Bennis, a renowned expert on organizational behavior, offers a similar emphasis in his book *Why Leaders Can't Lead*. He warns us to "guard against the crazies," saying that people's eccentricities and idiosyncrasies are okay but their neuroses are not.[1]

My book *Wounded Workers* was written to deal extensively with the leadership and the organization in three types of sick organizations: neurotic, addictive, and spiritually abusive.[2] In the present book, I am dealing with *wounded churches* and how to guard against the "crazies" in the congregation.[3] In Part I, I present the psychological dynamics of preexisting pathological—toxic—personal tendencies and dysfunctional family behavioral patterns that people bring into an existing conflict that often make the situation look worse than it really is. My main emphasis is, however, on when these people are actually the primary cause of the conflict in the first place, and I pay particular attention to spiritual warfare.

A unique aspect of this book is the emphasis on integration of the psychological and theological nature, causes and remedy of unhealthy church conflict. The primary focus is on the dynamic interplay of (a) dysfunctional family histories, delusional personal pathologies, and deplorable demonic influences that cause unhealthy conflict, and (b) the counteracting centrality of Jesus Christ and work of the Holy Spirit in the lives of victims of the conflict. The problem is unhealthy emotions and actions that are firmly established personality characteristics and troublemaking behavioral patterns learned through abnormal family histories—all of which open doors for spiritual warfare. The solution is resolution of unhealthy psycho-spiritual conflict through restoration of righteousness.

It is extremely important that we establish the priority of righteousness. I believe that for a church to be truly healthy she must first be restored to purity. Holiness trumps health. Holiness first, then wholeness. This bold claim is given biblical warrant by the fundamental relationship of the church to Jesus Christ. Every aspect of this book revolves around and gives top priority to the marriage relationship of *Christ and His bride*. The purity of the bride is the crucial context, and the restoration of individual righteousness and righteous reconciliation of relationships are the preferred biblical outcomes, for (a) researching the causes of conflict, (b) resolving conflict, (c) recovering from conflict, and (d) reframing the future after conflict.

The wide variety of types of conflict in the church is not my concern. Rather, my main focus is on rebellion. Having said that, *I must caution that we not treat every conflict as rebellion*. However, if it is rebellion we must treat it as rebellion, not something else. Rebellion in one form or another is at the root of all sin. Although not all conflict is sinful, rebellious conflict is. It is especially dangerous and harmful to the bride of Christ. A good example is vain argument for the purpose of promoting oneself and causing division. This is not conflict caused by mere disagreement, which can be very constructive and helpful to the cause of Christ. It is being quarrelsome, and it must stop:

> Don't have anything to do with foolish and stupid arguments, because you know they produce quarrels....Instead...[act] in the hope that God will grant them repentance leading them to knowledge of the truth and that they will come to their senses and escape from the trap of the devil, who has taken them captive to do his will.
> —2 Timothy 2:23–26

On a more personal note, I am sharing in these pages conflict situations that I have actually experienced. Personal experience is relatively subjective by nature and therefore potentially biased.

Consequently, I have tried to be diligent in presenting personal observations of publicly verifiable behavior—thereby adding a significant degree of objectivity to my analysis. As a psychologist, I hold firmly to *professional* standards of inquiry into the nature of conflict while being flexible enough to move beyond exclusively psychological categories of explanation. My role is like that of a forensic psychologist, offering a cogent interpretation of the conflict that is suitable for public debate. That is why I wrote Part I of this book: "Reality."

It is also natural for me to adopt a counseling psychologist role. That comes through in both parts of the book but primarily in Part II: "Choice." I move from asking, "What does it mean?" to asking, "What do we do next?" From analysis and critique to undertaking healing change and recovery. This involves a more *confessional* approach to the situation. I wholeheartedly acknowledge, as a fully devoted follower of Jesus Christ, my faith in the power of God through the leading of the Holy Spirit in understanding my own and others' experience of conflict and in the resolution of rebellious church conflict.

One thing I have concluded is that conflict is more than just conflict per se. In other words, conflict does not exist on its own. One cannot say, "The conflict made me do it." We all are responsible for the choices we make. I have also found that conflict is more than just political. It is always preceded by differing perspectives, differences of opinion, and diverse assumptions and expectations. That's called disagreement. It becomes conflict when someone decides to make a big deal out of it. Maybe because their feelings were hurt. They take offense at what someone said or did—or didn't say or do. They get angry, self-righteously angry. And they hold onto it and seek support for their cause. Pretty soon they're sowing discord, and rebellious conflict is on. It's not only about power and victory, either. It's also about personal validation and spiritual vindication. It's conspiratorial and crazy. One might even say possessed.

Conflict is not only about the politics of power but, perhaps even more so, about the management of personal problems. One thing is for sure: The choices we make in a conflict situation will depend on our personal perceptions of the reality of the situation. Throughout this book we face the dynamic of *different realities, different choices*. As we work our way through the material, here are some questions to get us started on the journey of finding peace while choosing to be sane in the insane circumstances in church conflict, choosing not to tolerate the intolerable, and choosing the calling the Lord has set before us:

- Is this conflict healthy or unhealthy?
- Is this conflict basically about systemic church problems or mismanaged personal problems?
- Is this just about leadership, or is it equally about followership?
- Is the most important issue hurt feelings or rebellion?
- Are we dealing primarily with human flaws and failings or spiritual warfare?
- Is this conflict fundamentally about broken relationships or sin?
- Is finishing well about success or faithfulness?

I have an abiding faith in *finding peace*, as both the motivation and the message—as well as the method—of resolving conflict in the church, rather than fearfully *keeping peace* or frantically *making peace*. These two are the most commonly discussed approaches, but they weigh too heavily on the side of human effort. Both can be equally superficial in their rush to eliminate uncomfortable conflict by either restraining negative emotions or repairing broken relationships. Peace is not just the absence of conflict. The danger lies in actually creating nonlasting pseudo-peace. I definitely prefer seeking the Lord's presence and His wisdom, recognizing how He is working in the midst of the conflict and joining Him.[4] Responding to conflict, especially unhealthy conflict, is not about flight or fight. It's about follow.

I have attempted to give a valid conceptual framework for understanding conflict and solid biblical guidance for finding peace in the midst of rebellious church conflict and resolving it in a way that gives glory to God. Indeed, the ultimate purpose for writing this book is to restore the holiness of the bride of Christ, which has come under attack, within the context of humility and conviction. Those who hope to resolve rebellious church conflict must invest their entire being in the manifold wisdom of God: He alone is God and there is none other.

I also want to say something about spiritual warfare. Unfortunately this is a broadly but only vaguely accepted intellectual concept. It needs to be more than that. The brute reality of spiritual warfare demands that we understand it as objective lived experience. One of the unique qualities of this book is the extraordinary account of actual sights and sounds of the battle. Another unique quality is showing specifically how demonic influence enters into the life of the church. It answers the question, How does Satan find entry points into unhealthy church conflict? It starts with open doors created by mismanagement of personal problems and disruptive behavioral patterns learned in coping with family problems. These are open doors for demonic influence to be brought into the church family through the psychological mechanisms (displacement, transference, self-deception) that created the unhealthy conflict in the church in the first place.

It helps to understand the biblical dynamics that underlie this whole process: "What causes fights and quarrels among you? Don't they come from your desires that battle within you? You want something but don't get it....[So] you quarrel and fight" (James 4:1–2). Conflict in the church is too often about selfish desires that cannot be met. So the inner turmoil is acted out by causing division and inflicting pain on others. This is not just an act of rebellion against individuals in the church but against the church herself. It is an attack against the bride of Christ!

The desires that battle within rebellious church members cause inner turmoil that is acted out in response to systemic flaws in the organization or culture of the church, or personality faults or moral failure of the leadership, or the mismanagement (craziness) of church members' own personal problems. This book is about the latter, summarized as follows:

1. Family problems, which become personal problems and are carried into the church, *manufacture* problems in the church

2. Personal pathologies and troublemaking patterns of behavior that are learned in dysfunctional families *mobilize* problems in the church

3. Demonic influences, which enter into the life of the church through open doors created by personal sin, *magnify* and *multiply* problems in the church

May God's grace be sufficient for those who remain faithful to continue to be fruitful in the face of the devastating emotional/mental/physical/spiritual personal damage caused by the troublemakers. May He also guide the faithful members in responding biblically to unrepentant troublemakers. And may the Lord have mercy on the wounded churches—the faithful churches that suffer from war within and do not lose hope.

Finally, a word to pastors. When war is declared on the church, i.e., against the policies and procedures and the leadership and faithful members of the church, pastors hopefully realize it is not about them (except in the case of serious sin, such as moral failure). But their tragic tendency is too often taking it personally and either giving up or fighting back. That they must not do. Pastor Chris Jackson, in a recent article in *Ministry Today*, shows pastors how to best serve as undershepherds of the flock in responding to unwarranted criticism in the church. Using Jesus, the Great Shepherd, as the pastors' model, he states:

> The entire ministry of Jesus was conducted against the backdrop of skepticism, negative questioning, challenges, rejections, betrayals and outright hostility—and He never let it deter Him from the Father's mission....He gives us a gritty example of how we can step up to the plate and preach and teach and prophesy right in the middle of criticism and opposition.
>
> Jesus...took time to relate with His disciples—He needed them personally...and He kept them close to Him even in His moments of deepest need. Pastor...are *you* close to anyone who truly

loves you and who has your back through thick and thin?

Even though Jesus guarded His heart and retained healthy boundaries, He was still able to love His own "to the end" (see John 13:1).[5]

In light of the strong possibility of personal problems being the root cause of many of the church's problems, you must continue to faithfully preach and teach the biblical perspective on murmuring, rebellion, and spiritual warfare. You must do so even in the face of hostile charges, such as you are "twisting" Scripture! And you are "embarrassing" some of us! Rest assured, if you are only reading directly from Scripture God's warning concerning His judgment and other dire consequences of causing division, such warnings will not be seen as out of place by those who are faithful members of the congregation. Also, the Holy Spirit can convict those who need to be convicted if they hear what God says in His Word, even if they take offense.

When you listen to faithful members with the gift of discernment of spirits as they recognize and report the presence of satanic strongholds in some in the congregation and demonic activity in public gatherings and personal relationships, you realize that Satan has declared war on the church. You are correct to take as your number one priority the protection of the flock against the undeserved pain inflicted on them by the wolves in sheep's clothing in their midst.

When you receive less than forthright (or no) support from officials in your denomination, who do not grasp the seriousness of the situation and do not understand the reality of spiritual warfare, it can be extremely frustrating. In addition, when they receive the complaints of and enter into conversation with those who are sowing discord and fail to enter into dialogue with you for clarification and constructive intervention—thereby aiding and abetting the development of discord and deception—it can be acutely stressful. And if you hire a consultant who actually makes matters substantially worse, you may feel that you are at the end of your rope. That is when you (once again) ask the Lord and those who "truly love you and have your back" to search you and know your heart, test you, know your anxious thoughts, and see if there is any wicked way in you (see Psalm 139: 23–24) that you need to correct through repentance and forgiveness. You need to deal with it, pick yourself up, and move on.

This is what the Lord wants you to do:

> Rejoice in the Lord always. I will say it again: Rejoice! Let your gentleness be evident to all. The Lord is near. Do not be anxious about anything, but in everything, by prayer and petition, with thanksgiving, present your requests to God. And the peace of God, which transcends all understanding, will guard your hearts and your minds in Christ Jesus.
>
> Finally, brothers, whatever is true, whatever is noble, whatever is right, whatever is pure, whatever is lovely, whatever is admirable—if anything is excellent or praiseworthy—think about such things. Whatever you have learned or received or heard from me, or seen in me—put it into practice. And the God of peace will be with you.
>
> —Philippians 4:4–9

Part I—Reality

Reviewing Underlying Issues

WHY DO PEOPLE get so riled up over issues in the church? Why does it get so personal? One possible reason is this. I've noticed over and over that when people have "stuff" going on at home, they seem to be quite volatile and quick to take offense at church. It's understandable because that stuff can be pretty heavy: a death in the family, financial trouble, a divorce in progress, spousal abuse, child abuse, an unwed teen pregnancy, a family secret, etc. The list is endless. These issues certainly can fuel and even create issues at church. Could that explain some of the meanness and self-centeredness of those causing division in the church?

Other questions concern the pastor. Why is the pastor so often the focus of personal attacks? Why does the pastor's personality so frequently become the target of the attacks? Again, I've noticed how easy it is to take offense at some personal characteristic or unintentional behavior of the pastor and "go to the mat" over it. It's rather odd that most pastor-related issues are just plain about personal feelings and perceptions.

The third component in any church conflict situation is the church herself. Why does the church get attacked so frequently? Why do people go nuts over issues ranging from the color of the carpet to the channels of communication? Once again, I've noticed how quickly people blame the policies and structures of the church for causing them grief. Suddenly, seemingly out of nowhere, there's a fury beyond belief developing into a "holy crusade."

Whether it's the people, pastor, or church, the issues are often seen exclusively as systemic, and all other possible avenues for inquiry into the problem are ignored or set aside. Seldom is serious consideration given to personal pathology and demonic influence explanations of church conflict. Seldom is serious consideration given to the possibility of satanic invasion as opposed to just leadership erosion or systemic implosion. And seldom is serious consideration given to the necessity of church discipline.

IDENTITY CRISES

These questions and observations are symptomatic of a much larger underlying issue: a profound identity crisis in both our pastors and our churches. This is challenging the very survival of our churches today. The numbers are astounding. The *LifeLine for Pastors* newsletter reports that as of 2002, 1,500 pastors per month quit because of burnout, contention in their church, discontinuity between expectations and reality, nonsupport from denominational officials, and moral failure—usually in some combination. Eighty-five percent said their greatest problem was dealing with disgruntled people. For 90 percent, the hardest thing about their ministry was dealing with uncooperative people. Four thousand new churches were starting up each year and 7,000 churches were closing, for a net of 3,000 churches closing annually.[1] More recently, *Leadership Journal* reported that 95 percent of the 506 pastors they surveyed had experienced conflict in their church. By far, the leading cause was control. Doctrinal and cultural issues ranked low compared to power and personal preference. In terms of church size, not only was control the number one problem in small churches, it became more widespread than in big churches.[2] Borrowing a famous line from the movies, "Houston, we have a problem!"

The identity crisis issue must be exposed, because it provides such fertile soil for people to displace their pain, anger, and fears from their traumatic histories and dysfunctional families onto their church.

Looking first at *the identity crisis of pastors*, I appreciate Bill Hull's insight in *The Disciple-Making Pastor* that helps distinguish between the disciple-making pastor and "the generic pastor."[3] In short, the distinction is between the priority of the former for church multiplication and the priority of the latter for church maintenance. The problem is that while most pastors sincerely and specifically want to make disciples to help fulfill the Great Commission and further the kingdom, they are pressured and pulled in the opposite direction. Success is defined in the generic terms of "bodies, bucks, and buildings." The generic pastor's role is defined in terms of the whims and wishes of the people he or she serves. In fact, "If [the pastor] places their felt needs first, he is considered caring; if he puts their real needs first, often conflicting with their felt needs, he is considered noncaring."[4]

Putting real needs first can be perceived as not only noncaring but also intimidating. That can be confusing to the pastor and disruptive to his or her sincere attempts at pastoral care. Consider the person who refuses to meet with the pastor because he or she is "intimidating" and "uses words," when in fact that person does not want to feel guilty and be held accountable when the pastor simply shares biblical truth. Or even without words the real complaint, when expressed honestly, would be, "Your very presence stirs up the darkness within me that I do not want to deal with!"

The church has become for the generic pastor a "crazy place" where the people tell him, in effect, that he's there for them, that his primary job is to please and placate them. That's what they pay him for. This role confusion is a problem, especially in the small church. In addition, it seems like practically everyone wants to have a say in making decisions about everything. This unbiblical demand for total democracy in the church is, according to Hull, "by far the most ludicrous means of [governing] ever invented, [and] makes leading the church almost impossible."[5] And when those who crave control defend their impatience as "from the Lord" and get nasty about it, their "holy harangues or accusatory verbal onslaughts... masquerade as a needed blast from the Holy Ghost. They [do not see their attacks] as spiritual pollution spills from [their own] unmet needs."[6]

The sad result of these various aspects of the generic pastor's role confusion/identity crisis is floundering around in an *"ecclesiological straitjacket."* The generic pastor desperately needs to be, as so refreshingly portrayed in *The Message*, "set free from the stifling atmosphere of pleasing others and fitting into the little patterns that they dictate" (Galatians 6:14).

The generic pastor's ecclesiological straitjacket is totally incompatible with the role of the disciple-making pastor: (a) creating an environment for making disciples, (b) establishing them in the faith, and (c) releasing them into the harvest to make disciples who make disciples. In other words, the identity of the disciple-making pastor is threefold: (a) *caretaker* of the vision of disciples making disciples, (b) *equipper* of disciples, and (c) *coach* of self-feeding, reproducing disciples.

I believe the role/identity of the generic pastor is not working, nor is it biblical. Pastors would do well to take a spiritual gifts assessment as a first step in addressing their identity crisis.

This will give them a clearer indication of God's will for them and how He can best use them in their calling to ministry. It will also help in alleviating some of the problems referred to earlier concerning the pastor frequently being the focus of personal attacks.

As a pastor, understanding your gift mix is essential for having an effective ministry. "Pastor" may not be your strongest gift. In fact, it often is not. I agree completely with Bill Hull on this point:

> Placing together the word *pastor* with the word *care* has led to some faulty thinking. For example, it concludes the person filling the office of pastor has pastoral gifts: showing mercy, help, encouragement, giving, and so on. The exact opposite is true; most people filling the office of pastor are gifted in leadership, teaching, administration, exhortation, and so on. They are not strong in traditional pastoral care areas. They do it because people expect it.[7]

This is precisely the point of contention I am driving at. Pastors feel like victims, not victors. I have heard many a pastor lament, "They just do not appreciate me for who I am. They're trying to force me into something I'm not and someone God never intended me to be." Satan uses that—here's that word again—like crazy. It is crazy, and helps explain why the pastor dropout rate is so high.

It is beyond the scope of this book to counsel what the pastor should take as a second step and then a third, and so on. Just let me say this: God gave gifts of service—including pastoral care—to the entire body, not just to the "pastor." It is your job to equip the saints for ministry. Remember that spiritual gifts are not given to anyone to build up oneself but for the Holy Spirit to use as Jesus builds His church. Gifts are not your identity but how you function biblically in the body of Christ. Gifts are not labels—they're how God is using you, not what you're called.

Take a second look at *all* the leadership gifts, seriously, as a pastor. Does your gift mix, for example, include some combination of an apostle gifting, a prophet gifting, an evangelist gifting, a pastor gifting, a teacher gifting? That's how God wants to use you in what He is doing: making disciples. That's your identity, pure and simple: disciple-maker.

Moving on to *the identity crisis of churches*, it can often be described as the tension between existing just for the church herself versus existing for mission. The basic difference is that missional churches exist for others, not for themselves. Church boards illustrate the difference. Many, if not most board members have never led a person to Christ, do not share a vision based primarily on the Great Commission and as Hull astutely observes, "by allowing the missions committee to allocate funds to mission projects…believe they are doing right by the Commission."[8]

Willow Creek Community Church outside of Chicago, for more than three decades a megachurch champion of the seeker-sensitive model, has recently gone through a significant identity crisis. As the result of an extensive three-year research project, they discovered that their attractional model was not effectively developing the spiritual growth of their members.[9] (See also my critique of big churches versus small churches in my book titled *All Churches Great and Small* referred to in the Introduction.)

Most shocking to the Willow Creek leadership was the realization that they had to rethink everything about how they do church. They had built their church around "The Church Activity Model for Spiritual Growth": Figure out what you think everyone needs and create programs to provide for those needs; then spiritual growth depends on increasing participation in those church activities. In other words, the more involved people are in the church, the more they become like Christ. The pain of facing the results, according to Bill Hybels, the Senior Pastor, was almost unbearable when they were told that involvement in church activities did *not* predict long-term spiritual growth—defined as increasing love for God and for others (Matthew 22:37–39)—either in attitude or behavior.

Two other discoveries in particular are striking. First, "The church is most important in the early stages of spiritual growth. Its role then shifts from being the primary influence to a secondary influence."[10] Continuing spiritual growth was found to be much more about one's deepening relationship with God than with the church per se. Church was perceived less as a place to go for Sunday services and building relationships and more as a platform that provides public service opportunities and support and encouragement of personal spiritual practices.

The other discovery that I want to focus on is this: "More than 25 percent of those surveyed described themselves as spiritually 'stalled' or 'dissatisfied' with the role of the church in their spiritual growth."[11] The *stalled* group had significant barriers to spiritual growth, it should be noted, that were personal in nature: life circumstances (divorce, death in the family, loss of job); addictions (alcohol, pornography, gambling); inappropriate relationships (adulterous, physically or emotionally abusive, cultish); emotional issues (depression, anger, fear); and gossip (being judgmental, being quick to take offense, sowing discord). As we shall see later, any of these personal challenges or pathologies can be displaced onto the church and in and of themselves cause conflict.

The *dissatisfied* group was comprised of the people who were most unhappy with their church and were also most likely to be considering leaving. Based on this research, we can expect one out of every ten people in most churches to be unhappy—and often extremely unhappy. In other words, don't be surprised if you discover that to be true in your own church. Just about everyone, however, will be surprised to learn that Willow Creek found that the dissatisfied people were the ones who were most committed to Christ and active in their church! Both stalled and dissatisfied groups provide fertile soil for conflict in any church, but one would not expect to see it sprout up among those who are most committed and most active.

As the research project expanded to other churches of varying geographic locations, sizes and ethnic and denominational backgrounds, they found the same pattern emerging. All churches need to take these findings under advisement. And as Willow Creek searches for a new identity, I would hope they do not restrict themselves to focusing on the issue of surface-level depth of spiritual growth, but that they will also seriously consider the issue of direction. If their vision and identity are based on revelation—the Great Commission—they will intentionally refocus the church outward, not just inward. I hope they will not just have a disciple-making program to provide service/evangelism opportunities and encouragement of spiritual practices, but that they will truly become a disciple-making church. More on that in Chapter 7.

Sick Organizations

When we ask the question, Does a "sick" church make people "sick" or do "sick" people make the church "sick"?, we have three places we can put the blame: the leadership, the church, or the people. It's never totally clear that we can blame one and not the other two. The best we can do in sorting out the craziness of the circumstances in church conflict is to discern the most pertinent truths of the reality that we perceive to the best of our ability. Often all three are in play, or so it seems.

In my book *Wounded Workers*, I present a detailed account of how all three options for blame can do a great deal of harm in three different types of sick organizations: neurotic, addictive, and spiritually abusive. I will briefly summarize each one and highlight two underlying issues to go along with an issue already mentioned for the leader (the ecclesiological straitjacket): for the church (spiritual subterfuge) and for the people (the unsanctified self).

The *neurotic organization* is often led by a charismatic leader who draws attention to himself through constant excitement and visibility. He is intolerant of ambiguity and is excessively focused on hierarchical, power-oriented control. He makes impulsive, grandiose decisions without adequate physical, financial, or human resources to support them. And although he works hard at impressing certain people, he desperately wants to be loved by all people.

The culture of the organization is inwardly focused on rules and regulations. Often there is an atmosphere of suspicion and distrust based on fear of potential external threats or internal catastrophes, such as a new church that might draw away members or differences of opinion that might cause some people to quit giving, making it more difficult to meet the church's financial obligations. The organizational culture is often highly politicized as well. There is an atmosphere of personal ambition, greed, and self-centeredness. Sometimes there is a competing group of malcontents—a "church within a church"—secretly holding meetings off-site to compete with regularly scheduled prayer and worship services, while conspiring for control of the church.

Other people tend to be unusually subservient and compliant and avoid taking responsibility for their own actions. Their sense of worth is often tied up in their perception of being personally connected with the pastor, and they compete with one another for his or her attention. They are devastated by a simple reprimand or even an unresponsive look or lapse of courtesy. Whether combative or compliant, we must remember that these people can make a church look neurotic because of their own neurosis, regardless of the healthiness of the church. This is especially true with people who are predisposed to jealousy in their relationships and distrust authority figures; who have a victim mentality and overreact when they don't get their own way.

We must also remember that sick churches don't get that way exclusively because of personal pathologies. Another cause is toxic systemic processes that permeate the entire organization. One such organization is the *addictive organization*. The addictive systemic process is most evident in (a) the sense that everything revolves around protecting the church and (b) a lofty mission that "hooks" everyone into feeling good even though they are in denial that they are not getting it done—they are furthering their own kingdom rather than the kingdom of God. Also, leaders and congregation alike define out of existence anything that threatens the future of the church or their illusion of personal safety and comfort—such as the reality of spiritual warfare in their midst.

At the individual level, people trust the promise that things will get better in the future, which is a powerful "fix" for relief from disturbing realities in the present. The power of the promise is "money in the bank" for the addictive church. For example, in times of trouble people may be told over and over that God is in control, which is a true statement and provides rock-solid reassurance that it will all turn out for the best. However, the reassuring promise can also provide fertile soil for codependence: helping those who are addicted to the secure future of the church and to her exalted mission to remain in denial regarding real threats to future success and recognition of mission failure. Again, pre-existing pathologies such as codependency that people bring to the situation can make it worse.

In the meantime the church thrives on the fix of the adrenaline high from workaholism that numbs people and nurtures their denial that they are just playing church. In effect, they are substituting the "spiritual high" from doing good works for God for actually experiencing God, and expecting Him to provide for their habit!

The third type of sick organization is the *spiritually abusive organization*. Here again, we see systemic processes that operate throughout the church. Leaders typically are preoccupied with their authority through calculated posturing and puffing up themselves at others' expense. They often position everyone in the congregation under the "mantle" or "covering" of their authority. They demand loyalty to the church and themselves, and they use their position to require the congregation to keep onerous rules and to live up to religious standards that they themselves never intended to observe.

Unhealthy faith in the pastor allows his self-proclaimed direct revelations from God to control the personal lives of members of the congregation. Disobedience of the pastor's pronouncements and a rigid corporate behavioral code is punished by a variety of shaming techniques. Living under grace is condemned as nothing more than being lazy or getting off the hook. To make matters worse, people find it next to impossible to leave the church, because they have been taught that it is safe only where they are, and it would be a grievous sin if they were to leave.

As with the other two organizational types, personal pathologies enter into and cause conflict in the life of the church. In the spiritually abusive church, these psychological problems add a potent new dimension to the circumstances in church conflict by opening doors for demonic influence. This influence causes spiritual abuse to operate in both directions between the leadership and the congregation. We need to take a much closer look at the spiritual realities behind conflict in the church. Are there patterns of anger, self-pity, being judgmental, being quick to take offense, jealousy, bitterness, hatred, unforgiveness, or besetting (constant, long-term) sin that have provided footholds for demonic activity in either the leaders or the members of the congregation? Has there perhaps been a history of arrogance, pride, self-promotion, and self-centeredness?

The questions are the same, whether for leaders or followers. Satan is no respecter of persons. He uses the same fault lines in everyone to provide footholds for influence in the lives of both individuals and churches.

Personal Strongholds

Where do we start in a conflict situation? When there is conflict the tendency most often is to zero in on the pastor. "If we could just get him to change—or leave—everything would be okay again." But we must all start with ourselves, whether leaders or followers. Get the log out of our own eye first! We then look at the doors we have opened for Satan to use to both harm ourselves and poison the church. We prayerfully consider how those footholds have become strongholds for demonic influence as moods have become habits, inclinations have become addictions, and moments have become a way of life.

Tom White, in his book *Breaking Strongholds*, describes strongholds as spiritual realities where demonic influence dominates "the *unsanctified self*—those parts of us not yet yielded to the Spirit or healed by grace."[12] What have we not yet yielded to the Spirit? Do we see any attitudes and actions in our lives that create ongoing cycles of defeat? Do we wrestle with negative self-talk concerning our personal worth? Do we struggle with fear and receiving God's love? Do we experience uncontrolled feelings of jealousy, pridefulness, unresolved anger, resentment or unwillingness to forgive?[13]

We also need to yield to the Spirit those strongholds that have entered into our life within the church and festered until the whole church has been poisoned. How have our personal strongholds caused *"spiritual subterfuge"* in the church? Is there discord and division within the body? Is there a pervasive feeling of distrust? Is there a cloud of confusion hanging over the congregation—recognizing that Satan is the author of confusion? Is there a battle for control of church governance?[14]

Is there strong evidence of *a destructive, rebellious crisis caused by the craziness of personal pathology and the spiritual subterfuge of demonic influence?*

These are the kinds of questions I will be dealing with in the remainder of this book. Questions will be addressed from both sets above, juxtapositioning the unsanctified self and spiritual subterfuge in the church. These questions will flesh out their causal relationship. My goal is to find a clear, unsullied path through the countless number of different realities and different choices for being sane in all the insane circumstances in church conflict, not tolerating the intolerable, and through it all finding peace.

Revealing Psychological Dynamics

Pastor Ed rose to share some passages of Scripture—all about praising the Lord. But as he began, a testy voice burst forth from the congregation: "We don't need any teaching!" Pastor Ed was taken aback, but not surprised. He had a reputation as an outstanding teacher, and he realized this was not just about his teaching.

A scene flashed back in his memory to a time not long ago during Sunday worship, when another voice blurted out, "You need to repent!" Pastor Ed was puzzled, not only about the words themselves, but also by the anger behind them. He thought, *There's no issue here of moral failure, financial impropriety, teaching heresy, or uncontrolled emotions.*[1] So, what's the problem? Then he remembered the recent confrontation behind closed doors when three women yelled at him for not being caring enough about some of their personal concerns. *This is crazy,* he thought. *What is going on?*

How does one make any sense out of this? It would be easy to conclude that it is just an authority issue, a social graces deficit or personality conflict, or any number of things. But it is not that simple.

Family Systems

Our usual approach in making sense out of conflict is through linear thinking: "A" causes "B." It helps us assign blame.

Sometimes we're right. For example, if the pastor commits adultery, or mishandles church finances, or preaches heresy, the problem is pretty cut and dried. But when conflict arises concerning personal perceptions of his personality characteristics or traits—perhaps some particular way he responds in certain kinds of situations—he is often still seen as *the* cause of the conflict.

Something else is happening. Something more complex. Something that is best captured by systems thinking applied to family systems: Members of the congregation are simultaneously involved in their own family systems and the church family system, and the emotional forces of the two interlock—unresolved issues in one produce symptoms in the other, so it works both ways. We should not always look at conflict or instability in the church as being singularly caused by poor leadership or unhealthy organizational structures. Rather, it is prudent and wise to seriously inquire into the unresolved family issues and emotional health of family members of those families in the congregation who are most antagonistic and hostile in participating in the conflict.[2]

Rabbi Edwin Friedman has written a classic and very influential book, *Generation to Generation*, which applies family systems thinking to churches and synagogues. His statement concerning the interdependence of family and nonfamily emotional systems profoundly describes the ripe-for-conflict atmosphere that constantly surrounds the pastor:

> With few exceptions, a nonfamily emotional system rarely achieves the same level of emotional interdependence as a personal family. The one nonfamily emotional system that comes closest to a personal family's intensity is a church or

synagogue, in part because it is made up of families, and in part because so much of the force of religion is realized within the family. What this means for the clergy is that we are constantly caught between counteracting forces of two separate but interlocking...systems, each of which is difficult enough to keep on an even keel much less to keep afloat when they are influencing one another![3]

In every church the corporate family and personal families are constantly interacting with one another. This emotional interface between the corporate family entity and the individual family entities in the congregation provides the context and inevitability of church conflict. Conflict is inevitable because, according to Friedman, "the intensity with which some lay people become invested in their religious institutions makes the church or synagogue a prime area for the displacement of important, unresolved family issues."[4]

Displacement

Simply put, displacement is relieving the anxiety, anger, hurt, and/or shame from things like financial difficulties, divorce, unresolved issues between a parent and his or her own parents, juvenile delinquency and/or, most especially, besetting sin by shifting all that negative emotion onto an issue at church—real or imagined—and in extreme cases turning it into a holy crusade. Or more simply, displacement is being mad at your wife and, to relieve your anger, kicking the dog.

Friedman cautions us: "Every time members of a congregation begin to concentrate on their minister's 'performance,' there is a good chance they are displacing something from their own personal lives."⁵ There is also a very good chance that when the focus is on new ideas or dissatisfaction with the way things are, the emotional intensity of the conflict is really a reflection of personal coping tendencies from dysfunctional families being acted out in the congregation. *More than likely, the destructive potential for the church lies not in the issue(s) per se but rather in the harmful emotional processes going on in the family or families most involved in the conflict and that are being brought into the congregation.*

Pastors must be careful not to accept displacement by getting caught up in the complaints and defending themselves against the claims of overwrought people. They must avoid becoming the exclusive target in the conflict, which if they "play the game" will only permit the troublemakers not to have to face themselves. Friedman notes that those who most actively promote conflict always assume that it is the issue that created the problem. "But it is the way they relate and think that gives any [issue] its inflammatory power. [They] *tend to overlook the cause of [their] misery by focusing on the object of [their] discontent*" (italics added).⁶

Family systems theory is especially helpful in debunking the tendency to blame the church for one's own problems. For example, there's a tendency to assume that the church mirrors people's problems back to them and makes them worse. "The pastor is too controlling, like it is at home, so it's unsafe for me to come to church," they often say. Therefore, the fault for the conflict does not lie with the brute reality of the person's own family but with the perceived reality of their church family. Or so they say.

Family systems theory also helps us understand dysfunctional families in the church that actually need a crisis in order to come together and pull together. A crisis enables family members, who have been emotionally conditioned for pain not peace, failure not success, to focus on and put their emotional energies into fighting a common enemy rather than each other. Therefore they create problems in their church family that mask their own dysfunction, so they don't have to take responsibility for and constructively work on their own problems. Sounds crazy, and it is.

Family systems theory forces us to consider that churches are molded by people's pathologies. They do not just mirror them, nor should the church be manipulated into simply masking the problems of dysfunctional families. No longer should these people be allowed to say with any credibility that the church is unsafe or dysfunctional and that's what made them do what they did. No, people are 100 percent responsible for their own behavior. Their problem is the unsafe/dysfunctional family they are living with, and we should not allow them to create a victim mentality to excuse their lack of responsibility and poisoning of the entire church.

Friedman concludes that the first question that should be asked in dealing with church conflict is, "Why now?" What recent changes have occurred in the emotional health of the key families participating in the conflict? The second question should be, "What opportunities are there to graciously focus these people on the unresolved issues in their own families and the disruptive behavior patterns of their family members?"

TRANSFERENCE

Displacement of important family issues takes many forms. Transference, a concept developed by the psychoanalytic branch of psychology, is the most pregnant with possibilities for describing the how, what, and why of displacement. It fills in the details and connects well with the topics of spiritual warfare, rebellion, and discipline. It also helps explain the emotional intensity that causes unhealthy conflict, where concerns become convulsions and rational discourse turns into irrational displays of negative emotions.

Transference refers to repressed painful memories, from an unresolved personal problem or abusive relationship from the past, which are transferred into a present relationship. It is a process of creating an interpersonal situation that resembles a traumatic reality of the past, acted out in ways that reshape and distort the reality of the present relationship. This is an unhealthy way of relating and usually is very confusing and destructive to the persons who are affected by it.

Transference in the church typically starts out as a petty, exaggerated complaint against an authority figure—most often it is a direct or indirect assault on the pastor. This is where it gets crazy, because these grievances are coming from an irrational and intense emotional reaction to something in the present that is unconsciously connected to emotional trauma from the past. Because of the unconscious connection between the past and the present (for example, rage against an unloving parent and anger at a perceived lack of compassion by the parent-figure pastor; or, hateful distortions of her relationship with her pastor and spiritual mother by a woman who has a venomous relationship of unresolved conflict with her biological mother), the present relationship will become a battleground for resolving the emotional pain from the past.

The built-up emotional force of the transference can easily become an illusory obsession: anything to avoid dealing with *the real conflict* from the past and the misinterpretations and sinful behaviors of the present. This makes an extremely important point, that "conflict" in the present is not real conflict. Valerie J. McIntyre, in her book *Sheep in Wolves' Clothing*, points out that people who do not understand the true nature of the conflict will commonly misuse the model presented in Matthew 18:15–17. She concludes: "The application of Jesus' teaching is inappropriate here. The real sin that needs to be confessed, and the real conflict that needs to be resolved, is not with the pastor but with someone from the accuser's past history."[7] In other words, "we" are not having a conflict!

Another common mistake in these cases, according to McIntyre, is focusing on communication to resolve the conflict, perhaps even calling in a mediator to help.

> For this model to succeed both parties must be objective and rational. But because transference is by nature subjective and irrational, the model will not work.
>
> In fact, the very act of calling in a mediator serves to validate the accuser's agenda. Furthermore, it gives the false impression that a conflict exists in which both parties are to share the blame....
>
> Thus, to involve a mediator before the transference is named can actually make things worse, particularly for the one receiving the transference. *In truth a mediator cannot help until the transference, and all the sins that issue from it, are acknowledged and confessed* (italics added).[8]

This is very good advice. The sins that issue from the transference must be acknowledged and confessed first, before reconciliation is pursued. This process is briefly outlined in

Appendix I for sheep dressed in the wolves' clothing of transference. It will be fully developed, for those who receive the transference, in Chapter 4. You can begin the process by kindly but firmly turning down all further requests to air grievances with the pastor (who is receiving the transference) and creating the boundary that all grievances must be aired only within the legitimate grievance policies of the church.

The idea of "sheep in wolves' clothing" is a profound insight into the inner workings of church conflict. It explains why people you care for and trust and who love and respect you suddenly turn against you. It is the devil's trap, a battle you cannot win with either attack or argument. Recognizing and understanding transference helps you to not take the rough treatment personally and to still love your rebellious sheep through all the confusion and pain caused by their crazy, cruel behavior.

Another profound insight is McIntyre's discernment of three key patterns when transference causes divisiveness and opens doors for demonic influence. First is the *Good Cause* pattern:

> Bringing discontented people together around an issue that seems positive and spiritual....The focus is generally along the lines of the leader's real interests. For example, a person might assemble people to talk about ministry to the poor, based on her authentic concerns. *The energy behind her efforts, however, will be the emotions of the unacknowledged transference, not the prompting of the Holy Spirit.*
>
> She will gather together some who are genuinely interested in the poor. But others, especially those also in transference, will participate simply

because they are attracted by the atmosphere of discontent....

Usually they fail to get any project up and running. Instead they succeed in galvanizing critical, judgmental attitudes toward the pastor, other leaders, or the church at large. Meanwhile, the person who drew the group together will be held in high esteem as one "having a heart for the poor." In contrast, the pastor's interest in the poor will be viewed as inadequate or feigned.

Unlike one who simply needs to let go of an idealized image of a pastor, the person in transference has a strong need to expose the pastor's inadequacies, whether real or imagined, to as many people as possible. *Behind this lies her anger at an inadequate parent and her need to forgive* (italics added).[9]

Second is the *Moral Crusade* pattern:

Persuading others to embark on a moral campaign to expose and confront a leader's flaws, whether real or imagined.... Singling out well-respected members of the congregation, he educates them through gossip and slander about the leader's "problems."...

For example, a man in transference launched a campaign against the senior pastor of a large church whom he believed had a problem with inordinate anger. *The man in transference had known terrible physical and emotional abuse throughout his childhood; the amount of rage he projected onto the pastor was therefore of unusual magnitude.*

Some whom he recruited were also in transference and jumped at the opportunity to air their grievances. But he also enlisted some who were well-meaning but naive, much like the two hundred men who went with Absalom to Hebron. These people hoped that their efforts would help the pastor to acknowledge his problem and secure the help he needed.

Little did they know that the one leading the campaign was in transference and therefore would be satisfied with nothing less than the leader's disgrace and removal from ministry....

Strangely, the person at the core of this type of group transference often goes unnoticed by the congregation at large (italics added).[10]

Third is the *Therapeutic Relationship* pattern:

Taking up a counselor's persona in order to "counsel" several people who are all in transference onto the same person....Here the one in transference takes on the role of a "counselor" toward those who have real or imagined grievances with a leader.

Often she will target a vulnerable person, initiating a conversation by asking leading questions that open the way for gossip and slander. With a few apparently benign queries, she can determine whether she has found someone who resonates with her grievances, all the while hiding her own heart.

For example, she might say, "Does it ever bother you that Rev. Jones never makes pastoral visits?" or "Have you ever had any trouble getting along with our minister?" She will wait to hear something that expresses her own feelings toward the pastor. Then, rather than empathizing in a way that would reveal her own hostility, she will say with concern, "I can see you are really in pain; Rev. Jones must have done something to hurt you," or "Others have reported this same thing to me."

She therefore feeds her counselee's discontent by reporting details from others' experiences that will further validate his or her angry feelings. In effect she helps her counselee take on her own grievances and those of others....

These situations have the appearance of being objective because of the counselor's ability to hide her emotions. In fact, they are completely subjective because the counselor asks questions and introduces information entirely motivated by her own emotions. *The counselee is manipulated into expressing the counselor's hidden feelings* (italics added).[11]

These three patterns give us an exceptionally well-detailed description of the dynamics of the transference process. We see the birthing of rebellion, the cunning and the corrupting influences on the entire congregation. We see the preparing of the soil for spiritual warfare.

I am most pleased that McIntyre is able to expose what I consider the most insidious technique for spreading divisiveness throughout the congregation. In the third pattern, called Therapeutic Relationship, she lays out step-by-step the deceitful manipulation at the core of the recruitment process. It goes basically like this: The "counselor" initiates conversations by asking leading questions (e.g. "Have you ever had any trouble getting along with our minister?"); then when the counselor hears something that expresses his or her own feelings toward the pastor, and without revealing his or her own hostility, the counselor says with concern, "I can see you are really in pain"; and finally the counselor reports details of other people's discontents (e.g. "Others have reported this same thing to me [and here is what they have said]") that will further validate the "counselee's" angry feelings.

The outcome is that counselees are subtly manipulated into expressing the counselor's own hidden feelings! I have one word for this: *guile*. Scripture is very clear in condemning guile (deception, deceit, cunning, trickery):

> "He that would love life and see good days, let him keep his tongue from evil and his lips from speaking guile; let him turn away from evil and do right; let him seek peace and pursue it. For the eyes of the Lord are upon the righteous, and his ears are open to their prayer. But the face of the Lord is against those that do evil."
> —1 PETER 3:10-12, RSV

A final note of caution: I have found that these people thrive in a small (cell) group environment. Their leadership breeds discontent, manipulates others to join an unhealthy personal agenda, and nurtures an elitist separation of group members from the rest of the congregation. Unhealthy small groups can cause tremendous damage to all churches, great and small!

Self-Deception

Self-deception is a fourth psychological dynamic in church conflict. In the context of unhealthy church conflict, self-deception is *the mismanagement of personal beliefs without pursuing the inconvenient truth of the matter*. It is closer to conscious, everyday lived experience than is transference. Accordingly, self-deception is somewhat easier to recognize. Appendix II lists some questions that can help in discovering one's own patterns of self-deception.

Gregg Ten Elshof's recent book titled *I Told Me So* is a wonderfully balanced, biblical examination of self-deception and the Christian life.[12] Often, according to Ten Elshof, self-deception is a *recasting of unresolved anger toward someone as concern, sadness, or worrying that someone else will get hurt*. Compounding the problem is the fact that others caught up in the same dynamic gravitate toward one another to reinforce their pretense that it is concern or sadness or worry that motivates them. I would definitely think twice before joining such a group. "The people with whom we surround ourselves are often complicit in our self-deception strategies. In fact, there are heights of self-deception only reachable with the help of others."[13]

This brings us to the phenomenon known as *groupthink*:

> Victims of groupthink tend to exhibit decreased moral sensitivity to actions and decisions which might otherwise present themselves as clearly out of bounds. This will be especially true when the group is united by a commitment to a big and seemingly righteous cause. The bigger and more urgent the cause, the more likely we are to be dead to the moral value of anything— or anyone!—perceived as standing in its way.

This seems to be especially true if the cause is "religious."[14]

Ten Elshof concludes that "what would present itself as obvious and egregious disrespect and mistreatment if considered alone is granted moral legitimacy by the group consciousness in devotion to a cause."[15] In other words, "cause does not justify."[16]

My conclusion is this: *Unhealthy groups produce unhealthy conflict!*

Now we turn to Chapter 3 to learn how unresolved family issues and unhealthy personal behaviors can be used by Satan to influence the life of the congregation. In Chapter 4, we will consider how to proceed when the troublemakers refuse to face themselves and their own contentious and pathological family and personal problems, and the damage they have caused to the bride of Christ.

Recognizing Spiritual Warfare

Conflict touches every part of our being. It gives us both headache and heartache. We can't eat and we can't sleep. It slows our step. It darkens our soul. But conflict also opens our eyes and ears. We can feel the entire weight of our burden and know the truth within it. It quickens our step and lifts our spirit.

Conflict also touches the cosmos. Conflict connects the visible realms of human activity on earth and the unseen realms of spiritual activity in the heavenlies. The connection is spiritual warfare. It cannot be emphasized enough that spiritual reality is *the* most important reality in the Christian's life. Spiritual warfare should be one of our top priorities, not to be evaded as an aberration but to be embraced as the Lord's work—normal, not abnormal. "For we are not fighting against people made of flesh and blood, but against the evil rulers and authorities of the unseen world, against those mighty powers of darkness who rule this world, and against wicked spirits in the heavenly realms" (Ephesians 6:12, NLT).

The problem is, committed Christians often can understand the concept but cannot grasp and accept the reality of the unseen spiritual realms. They show their confusion when they themselves become a manifestation of that reality under demonic influence, while they continue to claim that Satan cannot influence a committed Christian. How then do they have any hope of resolving conflict that is instigated and fueled by demonic influence? Paul clearly prepares us for the warfare they claim does not exist—at least for them: "We use God's mighty weapons, not mere worldly weapons, to knock down the Devil's strongholds" (2 Corinthians 10:4, NLT).

Before we can engage in spiritual warfare, we must recognize it. Francis Frangipane in his book, *A House United*, gives us some observable marks of a church under demonic attack:

1. "The confrontational attitude of [a dissenting group] in opposition to the established church authority."

2. Disregard by those in opposition for "love, church order and civility to obtain their desires." Frangipane points out that if single individuals were to engage in rebellious behaviors such as murmuring, slander and deception, they would be recognized and exposed as willfully sinning. But when they join forces, somehow they assume that these behaviors are justified because they are necessary for "fighting for a principle," and then they "enlist [more] allies in search of the truth"!

3. "Criticisms of the divisive group never let up; settle one issue and three more erupt."

4. "The issues that inflame [a splinter group] cannot actually be satisfied." They "use a smoke screen of religious issues to empower their cause: 'We just want more of God.'... [But] there is no need to divide the church to have more of God's presence,

especially since division itself causes God's manifest presence to withdraw!"[1]

In this chapter we will identify the observable behavioral manifestations—the specific biblical characteristics—that reveal the connection between the seen and the unseen realms. We will uncover preexisting pathological personalities and trouble-making patterns of behavior that are embedded in pernicious family histories and develop over time in response to abusive relationships, traumatic events, and besetting sins. These patterns of craziness potentially become strongholds of perverse demonic influences that fester and ultimately poison the entire body (referred to earlier as spiritual subterfuge).

Unsanctified Self

Francis Frangipane, in his profound little book titled *The Three Battlegrounds*, boldly proclaims, "Satan's first weapon always involves luring our eyes from Christ."[2] His first weapon is to draw us away from our first love, Christ Jesus.

Of course it's an incremental process that bit by bit destroys our life in Jesus. It's a battle for our soul, and yet we help it along in so many little ways. "Oh, it's okay for me to do this. I'm doing it for the good of the church." "This is no big deal. Everyone breaks the covenant." "I'm going to let everyone know what's wrong around here." And on and on it goes, the enemy having his way with us.

It all starts with the unsanctified self. E. Stanley Jones referred to a similar concept, calling it the unconverted subconscious. He was talking about those painful emotions connected to traumatic memories, unresolved broken relationships, and fearful anticipation of the future that we hold on to both intentionally and unintentionally. They remain over long periods of time "subdued but not surrendered," "cowed and suppressed, but not redeemed" until they blow their top.³ Frangipane details precisely how this unredeemed starting point plays a major role in spiritual warfare: "It is uniquely in our uncrucified thoughts and unsanctified attitudes that unclean spirits, masking themselves as *our* thoughts and hiding themselves in *our* attitudes, find access into our lives."⁴ There's a whole host of uncrucified thoughts and unsanctified attitudes that Christians express that open doors for demon-influenced patterns of behavior.

Taking Offense

Of all the weapons at Satan's disposal, the one that is most common and perhaps the strongest of all is taking offense.

I am referring to having a judgmental attitude toward someone's faults or weaknesses or perceived wrongdoing. This often leads to making a list of perceived offenses and harboring escalating, unresolved anger. The unresolved anger leads to malice (gossip) that leads to slander (calling names) that leads to self-righteous contempt that leads to condemnation. This is the lock-step progression of sin outlined by Jesus in the Sermon on the Mount. From the foothold of unresolved anger to the stronghold of condemnation.⁵

Scripture is clear:

> When angry, do not sin; do not ever let your wrath—(your exasperation, your fury or indignation)—last until the sun goes down. Leave no [such] room *or* foothold for the devil—give no opportunity to him. Let all bitterness and indignation *and* wrath (passion, rage, bad temper) and

> resentment (anger, animosity) and quarreling (brawling, clamor, contention) and slander (evil-speaking, abusive or blasphemous language) be banished from you, with all malice (spite, ill will or baseness of any kind).
> —Ephesians 4:26–27, 31, AMP

Dallas Willard in his book titled *The Divine Conspiracy* enlightens us a bit more about what we are dealing with here:

> Anger indulged…always has in it an element of self-righteousness and…a wounded ego. The importance of the self and the real or imaginary wound done to it is blown out of all proportion by those who indulge anger. Then anger can become anything from a low-burning resentment to a holy crusade to inflict harm on the one who has thwarted me or my wishes.…[6]

When we take offense and find fault in others in the body of Christ, "we are actually giving Satan the use of our mouths to accuse the saints before God!"[7] What a crazy mess this becomes. Conflict has entered into the unseen realms of spiritual activity in the heavenlies. We have entered into spiritual warfare.

Pathological Antagonists

Spiritual warfare is Satan's ultimate strategy for ravaging the bride of Christ and derailing the cause of Christ. Many Christians, however, do not acknowledge the possibility of satanic involvement in their personal or corporate lives. Some may acknowledge the power of darkness in external things such as cultural trends, living conditions, and natural disasters, but not in believers' personal matters and the body life of the church. In other words external yes, internal no.

To resolve the issue, first we must acknowledge that nowhere does Scripture state that a believer or the church cannot be directly influenced by Satan. Second, we would do well to heed Merrill Unger's conclusion in *What Demons Can Do to Saints*:

> It must be stressed that demons cannot indwell a Christian in the same sense as the Holy Spirit. God's Spirit enters a believer at salvation, permanently, never to leave (see John 14:16). A demon by contrast, enters as a squatter and an intruder and is subject to momentary eviction [when confronted with the blood and the name of Jesus]. A demon never rightfully or permanently indwells a saint, as the Holy Spirit does, and no demon can ever have any influence over any part of a Christian's life that is yielded to the Holy Spirit.[8]

As I have said before, it all starts with the unsanctified self. That is where the unclean spirits gain access to our lives. We have also looked at the unsanctified attitude of taking offense—a diabolically effective way to open doors to demonic influence in the church. Next we will consider the unsanctified behavioral pattern of pathological antagonism—a devastatingly destructive way for demonic influence to sow discord and cause rebellion and ultimately to close the doors of the church.

Pathological antagonism (toxic obstructionism) is a fight compulsively looking for somewhere to happen. It is arguably the harshest, most venomous, most spiteful, most ruthless, most hardhearted contributor to church conflict. That might sound too extreme, but for those who have gone through hostile, mean-spirited conflict, it is not. However, there obviously are different levels of antagonism in conflict situations.

Dr. Kenneth Haugk in his book, *Antagonists in the Church*, defines antagonists as

> individuals who, on the basis of *nonsubstantive evidence*, go out of their way to make *insatiable demands*, usually *attacking* the person or performance of others. These attacks are *selfish in nature, tearing down rather than building up*, and are frequently directed against those in a leadership capacity.[9]

Haugk expands on the key phrases:[10]

- Nonsubstantive evidence—merely suggestive or grossly misrepresented; claiming their delusional thoughts are accurate even though they are based on only a tiny bit of truth

- Go out of their way—quick to take offense themselves and triangulate others' hurt feelings rather than carry their actual burdens; hypersensitive (minor or unintentional slights are taken personally and responded to aggressively)

- Insatiable demands—never satisfied

- Attacking—it's all about control, no matter what the cost

- Selfish in nature—fighting for something supposedly for the common good, when their real agenda is something else that serves their own ambitions

- Tearing down rather than building up—the inevitable result is division ("Show me a divided and strife-torn congregation, and I will show you a congregation that has one or more antagonists in its midst."[11])

There is a multitude of ways to describe an antagonist. I particularly like Paul's description in 1 Timothy 6:4–5 (BERKELEY) of the person who "is conceited without understanding, with a morbid craving for controversy and a war of words, such as result in envy, wrangling, slander, bad suspicions [and] perpetual contention...." This moves us toward the extreme level of antagonism—pathological antagonism. The following characteristics are inspired by the literature and enriched by personal experience of the most destructive level of antagonism.[12]

Controlling tendencies—"straightening out" the church to meet one's own personal agenda; initiating a passive-aggressive, "wait-and-see" strategy of staying away from regular church gatherings—even organizing secret alternative meetings—because of "concerns" about the pastor and/or the church.

Aggressive tendencies—intimidating others by violating common rules of both decency and respect and defiling regular church gatherings (worship, corporate prayer, classes, business meetings) when they choose to attend; appropriating the role of intractable, intrusive questioner and contrarian—a constant fly-in-the-ointment.

Anti-social tendencies—not cooperating with established policies and community expectations; avoiding accountability.

Hysterical tendencies—exaggerating and dramatizing individual personally perceived offenses and concerns as catastrophic and together as constituting a major crisis (crisis-hallucinating); being hypersensitive to personal slights.

Narcissistic tendencies—displaying an excessive sense of self-importance; being preoccupied with admiration and attention from others.

I know what it's like to be in a church where a group refuses to meet regularly with the faithful members of the congregation. Where they disrupt and defile corporate gatherings. Where they show up unexpectedly with their critical demeanors, disrespectful comments, and intimidating outbursts—ranging from sudden, violent verbal attacks to storming out of meetings. Where they steal from the entire congregation the intimacy of corporate prayer, the joy of learning, and the sweetness of worship. Where they boycott observance of the sacraments of communion and baptism with the rest of the congregation. Where they secretly meet at other locations as a virtual church within a church. I know what it's like to be held hostage to rebellion!

Controlling Spirits

We have one piece left to fit into the spiritual warfare puzzle. Frangipane says,

> What governs the dissenting group is the manifest "power of darkness" (Luke 22:53). It is as though people invite the legions of hell to...find access to their secret resentments—the unresolved issues that exist in their hearts. Those things that are evil within human nature are fully awakened and...empowered by hell to fulfill every demonic gratification.[13]

The question is what do the demonic spirits actually do after they are let in by our *subversive attitudes* (unsanctified attitudes—e.g. a critical spirit and being quick to take offense) and when they act out through our *divisive actions* (unsanctified behavioral patterns—e.g. accusations and acts of rebellion)? I will focus on the most predominant category of spirits: controlling spirits.

There are three that stand out in unhealthy church conflict: the spirit of Antichrist, the spirit of Absalom, and the spirit of Jezebel. The *spirit of Antichrist* is a principality that is behind most church splits. It is a governing spirit that directs demonic warfare against the church and administers evil throughout entire geographical areas. We need not be confused by the Antichrist that will manifest in human form prior to Christ's return. The description of this individual in 2 Thessalonians 2 also describes the nature of the Antichrist spirit in its invisible form, which Scripture refers to in 1 John 2 and 4. Frangipane captures the full essence of the Antichrist spirit:

> The Antichrist spirit hardens the heart, keeping it from love. It nurtures unforgiving attitudes, causing those under its influence to splinter from a church due to various criticisms and minor doctrinal differences....
>
> It is simply "anti" Christ to justify unforgiveness, division and selfish ambition. *The Antichrist spirit will be disguised behind any number of issues, but those issues are simply tools this principality uses to divide the church.*[14]

People with the gift of discernment of spirits can sense the presence of the Antichrist spirit in an atmosphere that is not filled with holiness, but hollowness, in the aura of coldness and deadness that fills the room and in the scowl on the faces of those under its influence. This is particularly evident in a worship service of a church that has come under attack. But it does not mean that each person with a scowl on his face and mutterings in his mouth must be delivered from demonic influence.

It is important that we understand that this battleground is in the heavenlies. Ephesians 6:12 says that the principalities do not dwell in people but occupy the heavenly places, and Ephesians 3:10 declares that *through the church* God will make known His manifold wisdom (*one truth* in many forms: God is God and there is none other) to the powers and principalities in the heavenly places. Therefore, when the body of Christ aggressively agrees—in prayer, praise, and proclamation—with her Head in heaven that He is in us, the hope of Glory (another form of the one truth), the powers of darkness in the heavenly places are replaced by the Spirit of Christ. And the church is renewed by the fullness of the reign of Christ—on earth as it is in heaven![15]

Now the battle gets down to earth. In 2 Samuel 13:23–15:12, we read the story of betrayal of King David by his son Absalom. It is a story of taking offense, deception, and conspiracy. It has its apparent beginning in the murder by Absalom of his half-brother, Amnon. Then Absalom goes into exile for several years. It is when David allows him to return but refuses a face-to-face meeting with him that Absalom falls into the trap of taking offense. Nursing the offense, Absalom then pursues for several more years an agenda of self-promotion and deception that is the biblical basis for the *spirit of Absalom*.

Absalom is really full of himself, as he sits outside the city gate badmouthing his father's government as careless and uncaring. In addition, with perverted generosity and flattery he seduces the affections of the multitude and steals their hearts. He also recruits them to return to their districts and become ambassadors for his cause. Then he deceives David into giving him permission to leave Jerusalem and go to Hebron, supposedly to make a sacrifice, when in fact he intends to proclaim himself king. Two hundred men accompany Absalom, without a clue as to what he is up to. It is a well-executed conspiracy, indeed.

Beginning with the subversive attitude of taking offense, we can see how divisive actions can develop into the serious sin of rebellion against God's anointed leaders. Dr. Fuchsia Pickett, one of the most respected women of God in our time, describes exactly and completely in her book *The Next Move of God* how people under the influence of the Absalom spirit operate in the local church today and what the consequences will be:

> As Absalom stole the hearts of the men of Israel, so these flatterers learn to speak in such a way in the church that unsuspecting Christians begin to admire them. This admiration produces a spiritual pride in the deceived "Absaloms," who begin to believe they are more spiritual than their leaders.
>
> Then a competitive spirit takes over, and "Absalom" begins to misrepresent the decisions of the leadership and the direction they are taking. He (or she) sows strife and division and draws a group of people to himself. His followers feed off his critical spirit.
>
> After that, there arises a bold conspiracy. The "Absalom" justifies the actions of his group by focusing on the minor issues with which he found

fault in the leadership. Usually his accusations are not related to false doctrine or blatant sin within the leadership. Rather, he magnifies the imperfections or human traits of the leader.

Soon "Absalom" leads a naïve splinter group out to start a new church built on the foundation of offense. Since it is not built on the right foundation it cannot prosper. If the root of a tree is bad, the whole tree will be bad. So it is with every church that is founded on an Absalom spirit. It will be full of rebellion and disloyalty and will suffer continual church splits. God's judgment is on the rebellious church. [16]

Like the Absalom spirit, the *spirit of Jezebel* is self-promoting and consumed with desire for control. Like pathological antagonism, the influence of the Jezebel spirit is vicious and arrogantly rebellious.

The story of the Jezebel spirit begins with Queen Jezebel, the manipulative, rebellious wife of King Ahab. Frangipane describes her perfectly:

> Jezebel is fiercely independent and intensely ambitious for pre-eminence and control. It is noteworthy that the name "Jezebel," literally translated, means "without cohabitation."…Jezebel will not dwell with anyone unless she can control and dominate the relationship. When she seems submissive or "servant-like," it is only for the sake of gaining some strategic advantage. From her heart, she yields to no one.[17]

Jezebel is first mentioned in 1 Kings 16:31, regarding her marriage to Ahab. She is referred to again in 1 Kings 18:4, 13, and 19 as killing off the Lord's prophets and then inciting hundreds of false prophets. After learning that Elijah—God's true prophet—has killed all those false prophets, Jezebel promises vengeance (1 Kings 19:1–2) but does not succeed. Then in 1 Kings 21:1–23 we read about Jezebel directing that Naboth the Jezreelite be stoned to death so she can obtain his vineyard for her husband. So the Lord proclaims that dogs will devour Jezebel on that same plot of gound. The Lord also says, "I will avenge the blood of my servants the prophets and the blood of all the Lord's servants shed by Jezebel" (2 Kings 9:7).

Knowing she does not have long to live, Jezebel pridefully adorns herself and despisingly mocks King Jehu (2 Kings 9:30-31), who has arrived on the scene to carry out the word of the Lord. The "cursed woman" dies a ghastly death, and Jezebel's legacy as both a wife and mother is finalized: "Surely there was no one like Ahab who sold himself to do evil in the sight of the Lord, because Jezebel his wife incited him" (1 Kings 21:25, NAS); "'How can there be peace,' Jehu replied, 'as long as all the idolatry and witchcraft of your mother Jezebel abound?'" (2 Kings 9:22).

This is spiritual warfare both on earth and in heavenly places. It is between the spirit of Elijah and the spirit of Jezebel. As Frangipane portrays it:

> Each is the spiritual counterpart of the other. Is Elijah bold? Jezebel is brazen. Is Elijah ruthless toward evil? Jezebel is vicious toward righteousness. Does Elijah speak of the ways and words of God? Jezebel is full of systems of witchcraft

and words of deceit. The war between Elijah and Jezebel continues today.[18]

Jezebel is mentioned again in Revelation 2:20 in the letter written to the church at Thyatira. Here we have a situation where the symbolic Jezebel is to the church at Thyatira what Jezebel, Ahab's wife, was to him. In the former the specific evils referred to are immorality and idolatry. In the latter, I have already cited the specific evils of witchcraft and idolatry listed in 2 Kings 9:22. Most people would agree on what idolatry means, but it might be helpful to look a little closer at immorality and witchcraft. Certainly sexual immorality is clearly stated in the biblical reference, but the larger issue is most likely control through any and all means of seduction. Similarly, witchcraft in the spiritual context of the passage is a "counterfeit [of] true spiritual authority by using domination, manipulation, intimidation and control over other believers."[19]

Drawing primarily on the work of John Paul Jackson in his book *Unmasking the Jezebel Spirit*, I have compiled the following list of 15 unsanctified behavioral characteristics of people who could be influenced by the Jezebel spirit:

1. Being insecure, prideful, and dominating with a consuming desire to control.

2. Being threatened by and despising authentic intercessory prayer (this sets people free!) and anointed prophesy (Jezebel cannot control true prophetic anointing).

3. Seeking to gain the reputation of being uniquely spiritual by conjuring up "prophesies" and a "word

from the Lord"—which do not pass the biblical test (see Chapter 8).

4. Overly exaggerating their actions and unnecessarily dramatizing their orations in a calculated attempt to establish a reputation as a passionate discerner of the truth.

5. Manipulating people's fears by weeping or hyperventilating over invented calamities, and triangulating others' self-perceived hurts (rather than real burdens) simply as a ruse meant to promote themselves as deeply caring Christian persons.

6. Forming strategic affiliations by recruiting people who are perceived by others as spiritually mature or influential with others to gain support before showing their hand.

7. Seducing an influential person in the congregation into an emotionally dependent, magnetic, soul-sister or soul-brother relationship to gain leverage in the congregation.

8. Avoiding accountability by secretly engaging others with hurtful innuendoes, false charges, false teaching, and false prophecies that cannot be directly challenged.

9. Justifying their actions with comments like, "I'm just concerned about what's best for the church" or "I am only doing what God has told me to do," or rationalizing their brazen behavior with confusing spiritual language and misleading or inaccurate Bible references.

10. Undercutting spiritual authority by arrogantly elevating their own ideas about the church above the pastor's and sharing their concerns with others in the congregation first instead of following the biblical pattern for sharing grievances.

11. Being jealous and disdainful of spiritual authority—in the extreme case impetuously boasting, "We don't need a pastor!"

12. Seeking to gain the approval of others by publicly flattering the pastor, then getting jealous of the image they have built up of the pastor and trying to take him or her down.

13. Zeroing in on the pastor to find alleged weaknesses and personality flaws that can be exploited to remove him or her and gain control of the church.

14. Relentlessly pursuing a nefarious personal agenda of base accusations against the pastor and enlisting in their holy crusade any who will agree.

15. Taking copious notes at inappropriate times to record the pastor's every word and move in minute detail for possible new ammunition for the battle ahead.[20]

What can we glean from this list? First, we have examples of the chief characteristics of the Jezebel spirit:

- Consuming desire for control (1)
- Hatred of intercessory prayer and true prophesy (2)
- Manipulative and deceptive self-promotion (3–5)

- Contempt for anointed spiritual authority (10–11)
- Relentless pursuit of a wicked personal agenda (12–15)

Second, we can see the very deliberate, systematic development of demonically influenced rebellion:

- Self-promotion (3–5)
- Gathering strategic support and influence (6–9)
- Challenging spiritual authority (10–11)
- Bringing down the anointed leadership of the local church (12–15)

Restoring Church Purity

Rebellion

When the Jezebel spirit enters into a person, rebellion is at the core of his or her being. Rebellion becomes the issue. Demonic influence, however, is not always the cause of rebellion. Nor is rebellion the cause of every conflict in the church. Nevertheless, I am convinced that rebellion—with or without demonic influence—is at the center of most church conflicts. And no church, no matter how great or healthy or pure, is exempt from rebellion!

Rebellion must be dealt with. Biblically, rebellion has many forms. I will consider three: sowing discord, lawlessness, and witchcraft. Starting with *sowing discord*, we get a very clear picture from Scripture of how God feels about it:

> A worthless person, a wicked man is he who goes about with a perverse [contrary, wayward] mouth, signaling [his] true intentions to [his] friends by making signs with [his] eyes and feet and fingers. Willful *and* contrary in his heart, he devises trouble... continually; he lets loose discord, *and* sows it. Therefore upon him shall the crushing weight of calamity come suddenly... without remedy.

> There are six things the Lord hates—no, seven things he detests:
>
> - A proud look...a lying tongue, and hands that shed innocent blood....
> - A heart that manufactures wicked thought *and* plans, feet that race to do wrong, a false witness who pours out lies...and he who sows discord among his brethren.[1]

Of all that the Lord hates, sowing discord is the worst! This is not just a list of seven reprehensible sins. One stands out from the rest, as clearly explained in *The Wycliffe Bible Commentary*: "These are not seven cardinal sins.... [Rather,] the proverb is climactic. The [first] six items are background for the seventh, which receives the emphasis (cf. Job 5:19; Prov. 30:18–19). The statement emphatically concludes with what verse 14 had introduced—['soweth discord']."[2]

The entire passage is meaningful to me. I have vivid recollections of church conflict with much of the background material in this passage: contrariness, signaling true intentions to allies with a glance, grimace, or gesture, willfully causing trouble, putting on that frosty proud look, conjuring up wicked thoughts and plans that defile the church and profane the name of the Lord, and deceitfulness—in short, sowing discord among the brethren.

Another form of rebellion is *lawlessness*. According to Jackson, since God has placed all authority in position, attempting to launch a revolt against pastoral authority is lawlessness against God.[3] Ken Sande, president of Peacemaker Ministries, agrees in his widely acclaimed book *The Peacemaker*: Although submission to authority is not a popular concept in our society, "those who rebel against biblically established authority are rebelling against God himself (Rom. 13:2)."[4] He reminds us, however, that authority has its limits. For instance, no one in authority has the right to instruct you "to do something that you believe is unwise, unfair, or sinful."[5] That is an essential point to make, as is this one:

> Respect for authority is so important that Jesus commands us to submit to those over us, even when they behave hypocritically or harshly (Matt. 23:1–3; 1 Peter 2:13–3:6). In other words, God calls us to respect the *positions* of those in authority even when their *personalities* leave much to be desired.[6]

The story of Korah in the Old Testament gives us another example of the unpopularity of God's authority structure in our postmodern world. In Numbers 16 we read that Korah is conspiring with two others to incite a rebellion against Moses. They, along with 250 other prominent leaders, go to Moses and Aaron and criticize them for assuming too much authority. Their rationale is that everyone in the congregation is holy and the Lord is present with each and every one of them. Therefore they ask, "What right do you have to act as though you are greater than anyone else among all these people of the Lord?" (Numbers 16:3, NLT). In other words, the people rule, and we want all decisions to be made by consensus.

Moses responds by challenging Korah and his followers that it isn't enough for the Lord to have separated them, as Levites, from the rest of the Israelite community to do His work in the tabernacle and minister to the larger community. Being near to the Lord is not special enough for them. Now they want the priesthood as well! Their rebellion, Moses warns them, is really against the Lord. This is a strong reprimand of their usurping of God-given spiritual authority.

Then it gets interesting. It goes from reprimand to wrath. Korah causes further trouble by stirring up the entire community against Moses and Aaron. God responds by causing the earth to open and swallow up Korah and his men, with their households and all their possessions, demonstrating in no uncertain terms that He has called Moses to lead His people. Their rebellion is in contempt of the Lord Himself. Then fire comes forth from the Lord and consumes the 250 leaders who originally followed Korah. And the next day the whole Israelite community that Korah had stirred up blames Moses and Aaron for the wrath of God the day before!

God responds one more time. He sends a plague to put an end to the throng gathered in opposition to Moses and Aaron. Moses tells Aaron to take his censer and run into the midst of the people and make atonement for them. The plague stops. The final result is close to 15,000 people dead because of one man who recruited other leaders of the faith community and stirred up the entire community to rebel against God's appointed leader.

It's awfully arrogant for some people to believe that revolt against spiritual authority per se is something God would ever condone. If there's a problem, there certainly are other options that would honor His name and give Him glory.

Francis Frangipane gives good advice for what people can do when they are dissatisfied with the pastor's performance or perceive that he has some sort of problem other than serious sin—"serious sexual sin or crimes worthy of imprisonment."[7] Perhaps he rubs some people the wrong way—perhaps he's too controlling. But they must ask themselves if their own "wrong attitudes toward authority cause [them] to misjudge a leader as 'controlling' when he is, in fact, simply fulfilling his God-given spiritual responsibility."[8] Or perhaps he's not doing his job the right way. Again, they must ask themselves if they actually mean not the way they would prefer. Frangipane's advice is be like Jethro, who was humble and caring when he shared his concerns with Moses (see Exodus 18:14), and do not be like Korah who was filled with ambition and rebellion when he confronted Moses with his.

Similarly, when you have legitimate concerns about the church, "instead of manipulating the unmet needs of the church to gain a following [as Korah did], submit yourself and your talents to the church leaders. Ask them how you can help. Do not exploit the needs; help meet them."[9] Then you can "give advice, but then let them administrate as they see fit."[10]

Finally, 1 Samuel 15:23 equates rebellion with *witchcraft*—defined earlier as a counterfeit of true spiritual authority by using domination, manipulation, intimidation, and control over other believers. It is accomplished with the assistance of demonic spirits. Witchcraft is imposing one's will by manipulating others, but Jackson is quick to point out that "manipulating others does not make an individual a witch....Nor does it mean the individual is a practitioner of magic....But it suggests that a person is masking his or her true intention."[11]

Purity

The true intention of those in rebellion is to impose their will while claiming they are only doing God's will. But, Jackson warns:

> They are not in touch with their own rebellion that blinds them to what God is doing. Those who practice manipulation in their homes and in personal relationships will do the same in church settings, unless [it] is corrected. For a church to flourish, however, control and manipulation must cease.[12]

That's it in a nutshell. Those who practice these things at home will do the same thing in the church, and it has to stop! It must be corrected with corrective church discipline. Sounds simple, but it is not. This is where it gets complicated.

Let me explain. First, for years the main emphasis of all the books, seminars, and seminary courses was on church growth. Then, more recently the focus has shifted to church health. Now, I wholeheartedly believe we are due for another major shift in our priorities, to church purity.

The church is the bride of Christ. Therefore, the church needs to be healthy, and above all else she needs to be pure. I believe holiness trumps health. Holiness first, then wholeness. To be truly healthy, a church in conflict must be restored to holiness. God's house is a holy house, and where there is purity there is peace. Let us shout to the Lord with praise and thanksgiving in our hearts, "Holiness is the mark of Thy house" (Psalm 93:5, BERKELEY).

Second, a decision needs to be made at the front end of dealing with church conflict. Is the fundamental problem in church conflict situations generally broken relationships or is it sin? More specifically, is the key to conflict resolution (a) reconciliation of broken relationships and (b) restored community? Or is it (a) restoration from sin and (b) righteous reconciled relationships and corporate righteousness?

I believe that in our postmodern world we have lost our way in the church. In our craving for community we have forgotten the biblical primacy of righteousness. We would rather kiss and make up for the sake of unity-at-all-cost. We would rather sing *Kumbayah* and end up with unrighteous reconciled relationships for the sake of the appearance of togetherness—instead of true reconciliation between a people made holy and God!

Craving for community has another problem that interferes with dealing with rebellion: a built-in yearning for consensus. This is governing by the will of the group. The church at Laodicea is an example of the postmodern church that is consumed by her longing for consensus. The name Laodicea actually means "the people rule." Jesus says to the church at Laodicea, "I know you inside and out, and find little to my liking. You're not cold, you're not hot…!You're stale. You're stagnant. You make me want to vomit" (Revelation 3:15–16, The Message).

Laodicea is the only church of the seven churches that Jesus addresses where He is on the outside trying to come in, saying any *one* who will hear His voice and open the door to Him will enjoy His presence. We see in Scripture then, that rule by the people is unbiblical, and the presence of the Lord is unwelcome. In addition, unyielding commitment to consensus produces a culture based more on personal relationships and feelings than on ministry results and a vision for furthering the kingdom. It reduces the pastor merely to a facilitator and resource person.

Consensus plays right into the hands of those who are in rebellion. The weakened leadership creates an environment that allows confusion and fear to escalate and make the conflict much worse. Further, the inability of weak leadership to act as a circuit breaker to de-escalate the conflict gives those who are most intensely involved in the rebellion an added advantage.

Now they can play the "We'll leave if our concerns are not met" card. Now they can blackmail those who crave unity at all cost to "reconcile" with them and their agenda.

To keep from being held hostage to their demands, the congregation and leadership must distinguish between togetherness and stuck-togetherness and refuse to continue to pander to the forced solidarity of pseudo-community at the expense of the integrity of the vision.[13] Vision trumps community. When the church gets that right, she is much better prepared to take the necessary next step: corrective church discipline.

Discipline

Corrective church discipline is the hinge that opens the door from pain (Part I) to peace (Part II). It restores holiness and leads the church back to wholeness.

First we need to put church wholeness or health in perspective. If we have conflict in the church, do we have an unhealthy church? This is an important question, because people like to say when there's conflict that the church is unhealthy. When things get ugly, the church is the cause. The church is unhealthy and therefore the problem. I oppose that view. When the conflict is unhealthy—when people are deceitful and hurtful in their use of conflict for personal gain—*unhealthy conflict* is the issue, not a symptom of something else. Unhealthy conflict is the problem in and of itself. The church is not the problem. If, however, the conflict is healthy and the church is already infected by immoral or illegal acts of the pastoral leadership and/or corrupting corporate systems, she is most likely sick.

Something must be done. The leadership must be redemptively disciplined and/or the corporate systems must be redeemed. In the case of the latter, all corporate structures (e.g.

governing policies, financial procedures, patterns of meeting for worship, prayer, fellowship, etc.) and every systemic process (pattern of thought and action, as well as form and method of organization) must be intentionally brought under the lordship of Jesus Christ. I go into this in much more detail in my aforementioned book *Wounded Workers*.[14]

Unhealthy conflict does not in and of itself determine health. Whether a healthy church gets bit by a flu bug or is corrupted by a deadly disease (so to speak), and regardless of the cause (for example, personal pathologies embedded in dysfunctional family histories, unredeemed corporate structures and systemic processes, or spiritual warfare), a faithful, healthy core of people almost always remains in the congregation. I firmly believe that Jesus will continue to build His church through these people. Satan, on the other hand, tells the church that every flaw is a fatal flaw and that she is totally sick and worthless, hoping every one will lose hope and give up. But the Holy Spirit reveals the corrupting sin to the faithful core and empowers them to eradicate it. If the conflict is unhealthy, the faithful core—the actual healthy church—as she is led by the Spirit to pray and praise Jesus through corporate prayer and worship, will be able to defeat the enemy in whatever method he chooses in attacking the bride of Christ. And the healthy church will prevail against the gates of hell (see Matthew 16:18)!

Holiness is the fundamental key to church health. A pocket of sin must be eradicated, or it could spread like cancer throughout the entire body. When it does begin to spread, we have two choices: prune or placate. Corrective church discipline is a pruning strategy, based on the corrupting reality of sin.

The alternative is based on a different view of reality: broken relationships. The goal is restored fellowship. A well-articulated presentation of this model is provided by Jim Van Yperen, founder of Metanoia, a Christian consulting business for intervention in church conflict, in his book *Making Peace*.[15] I have pulled together his ideas into the following:

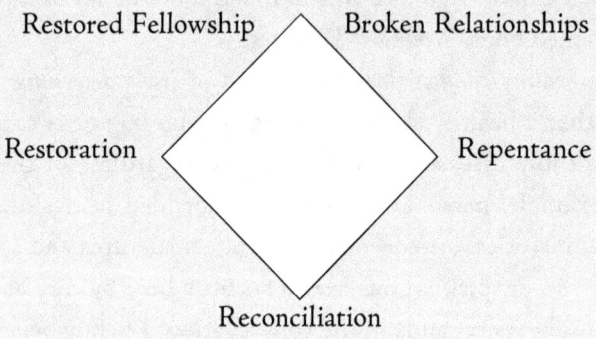

These are the steps: reconciliation, through repentance, for restoration of fellowship. In other words, broken relationships are reconciled through repentance, which restores corporate fellowship, which establishes authentic community. We could refer to this as the Authentic Community Model.

Standing in sharp contrast is the corrective discipline approach, where sin is seen as the true cause of conflict and broken relationships are seen as a symptom. The goal is restoration of righteousness. An outstanding presentation of this model is provided by John White, a renowned Christian author with worldwide ministry, in his book co-authored with Ken Blue, *Church Discipline That Heals*.[16] Here is a summary of their ideas:

Restoring Church Purity

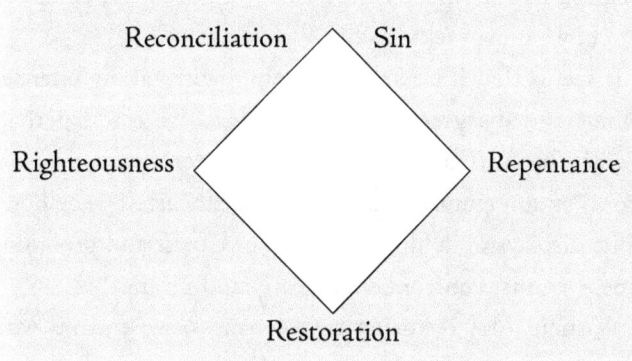

These are the steps: restoration, through repentance, of righteousness for reconciliation. In other words, restoration of individual righteousness is achieved through repentance, which makes righteous reconciled relationships possible, which restores church purity. We could call this the Church Purity Model.

Both models are biblical approaches, so the choice to be made is not one of either/or but rather which one has biblical priority over the other. Both authentic community and church purity are necessary for a healthy church, but the question is where do we start in resolving church conflict? And what are we trying to restore, fellowship or righteousness? The choice is clear: righteousness first, reconciliation last.

The Authentic Community Model places great emphasis on reconciling broken relationships as the starting point, followed by a consensus decision-making process for organizational change. Only within the context of reconciliation and systemic change, it is claimed, can sin be redemptively exposed. Not so, say White and Blue: "We cannot wait for radical changes in churches before we deal with sin. Sin flourishes among us, clamoring for correction. And though we recognize that corrective discipline is but first aid for the wounds of an undisciplined church, we must tackle it first."[17]

It seems that if we are just dealing with taking offense, hurt feelings and disagreements about ideas, we could perhaps get by with the Authentic Community Model. But if we are in the throes of antagonistic, arrogant, hardhearted rebellion with public displays of defiling the body of Christ and profaning His name, we must confront sin directly and promptly.

Without first restoring righteousness, we end up with unrighteous reconciled relationships. If the sin of rebellion is not dealt with, reconciliation is just a series of forgiving one another's offenses and asking for forgiveness for hurting someone's feelings. We need to be restored to righteousness individually and then reconciled with one another, in White and Blue's words, as "a people-made-holy" before God.[18] We must first and foremost come back to God individually and corporately, not just come back into fellowship with one another. Restore righteousness first, then reconcile relationships. Get right with God first, then with other people.

The Church Purity Model incorporates church discipline that is both corrective and restorative. The big picture—the preferred reality and choice to be made—is soundly portrayed by White and Blue:

> Restoring sinners is not only a classic aim of corrective church discipline, it is also a [basic] biblical aim. Restoration takes place when sinners are brought back to righteousness. They repent....Rebels see their folly and wrongness and abandon their insurrection....
>
> [We are] primarily concerned with the righteousness of Christ's body....For fellowship to

be re-established with a brother or sister (reconciliation), the church must be pure. And for the church to be pure, individuals must be made pure (restoration).

Restoration thus opens the door to reconciliation. The former rebel becomes a friend again.... The once [sowers of discord] resume their roles as integral members of a healthy community....

Thus to be restored means more than to have repented and been forgiven. Sin damages. It weakens resistance, dulls conscience, debases appetites, brutalizes instincts. It is habit-forming and character-changing. Sinners need to be healed and rehabilitated. We do not use the word *restoration* to refer to being restored to fellowship. Rather *restoration* means being brought back to the holiness one held before a fall.[19]

The reality we face when insurrection infects the church is the recalcitrant lawlessness of the few. It is an unruly defiance of authority that is not just going to go away. Rarely are the lawless actions of the leaders of rebellion merely circumstantial. Fundamentally they are characterological. We are dealing with enduring personality characteristics that are not readily amenable to change and must therefore be addressed directly by church discipline. This is especially true for pathological antagonists. Almost without exception they have caused trouble in their previous churches and will do so again, and again, and again. If we do not face the right reality and make the correct choice for the future, they will, without a doubt, concoct some other issue and come at us again!

The choice we must make is to restore individual and corporate righteousness. The reality of sin trumps all other realities and makes corrective/restorative church discipline the clear biblical choice for resolving rebellious church conflict. We must rehabilitate the rebels through a process of healing that will bring them back to holiness and allow them to once again be integral members of the healthy community. Peaceable reconciliation based on righteousness is our ultimate goal. Master theologian and prolific author G. Campbell Morgan said it well many years ago in *A First Century Message to Twentieth Century Christians*: "God's order is the order of peace, but it is always peace based upon purity, for the wisdom that is from above is first pure and then peaceable."[20]

Part II—Choice

Resolving the Conflict

We have before us a death-in-the-kettle scenario. In 2 Kings 4:38–41, we read that there was famine in the land. Elisha made provision for freshly boiled stew in a big kettle. But when the men began to eat, they cried out, "There is death in the kettle," and could not eat from it. Elisha said, "Bring me some flour," and when he threw it into the kettle nothing harmful remained. The flour was symbolic of God's power to remove the poison. He can do that today, in our churches, in the midst of conflict.

When we face rebellion in our church—death in the kettle—we need to ask, "Lord, what can we add to pull out the poison and give us peace?" I believe the answer lies in the title of White and Blue's book *Church Discipline That Heals: Putting Costly Love into Action*—loving confrontation that leads to restoration of individual righteousness, reconciliation with others, and church purity.

Confrontation

Corrective/restorative church discipline is a process of loving confrontation of sinful behavior, within a biblical framework. The *context* is commitment to biblical principles for the peaceful life of the body of Christ:

- Working together to further the kingdom

- Working together to advance the church in holiness
- Participating together in regular worship and celebration of the sacraments
- Contributing time, talents, and treasure faithfully in support of the ministries of the church
- Caring for one another in Christian love
- Being slow to take offense, quick to forgive, and always ready to reconcile
- Avoiding all appearances of evil

All people in the body of Christ are expected to seek to be morally pure and to live at peace with one another. Seeking to divide the church rather than promote the unity of the church will not be tolerated. Unity is the essential context for loving confrontation. Therefore, we must promptly address the brute reality of the sin of rebellion.

Some, however, would say that "all sins are equal" and must be dealt with at the same time. That is absurd. Individual differences of opinion and hurt feelings, even unintentional offenses, are not on a par with a small group of dissenters intentionally seeking to divide the congregation, breaking the covenant of membership, and thumbing their noses at gathering on a regular basis with their brothers and sisters in Christ.

Willful sin that harms the entire body of Christ must be dealt with first. The faithful, healthy core of the church that is being held hostage to the troublemakers, never knowing when they'll show up and what they'll do when they do show up, must move on. Prune, don't placate. Show them tough love, not the enabling behavior they are used to receiving at home. Don't let them excuse their disruptive behavior with what they get by with in their own families: "It's okay. They'll get over it."

On the contrary, Paul clearly tells us not to just "get over it." Following are several of his bold statements that give the flavor of his context of disruptive behaviors and appropriate disciplinary action.

Having an "unhealthy interest in controversies and quarrels... that result in envy, strife, malicious talk, [and] evil suspicions" (1 Timothy 6:4).

Being "hard to deal with and hard to bear...self-centered...proud *and* arrogant *and* contemptuous...abusive (blasphemous, scoffers)...unholy *and* profane...relentless—admitting to no truce or appeasement...false accusers, trouble makers...treacherous (betrayers)....Avoid [all] such people—turn away from them" (2 Timothy 3:1–5, AMP).

Causing division—"Watch out for those who cause division....Keep away from them. For such people are not serving our Lord Christ, but their own appetites. By smooth talk and flattery they deceive the minds of naïve people" (Romans 16:17–18).

Being "disorderly... [and] being busy with other people's affairs instead of their own.... Do not associate with him... [but] do not regard him as an enemy.... [However do] admonish and warn him" (2 Thessalonians 3:11, 14–15, AMP).

Claiming to be a Christian, but having "a foul tongue (railing, abusing, reviling, slandering)" (1 Corinthians 5:11, AMP).

> Don't you realize that if even one person is allowed to go on sinning, soon all will be affected? Remove this wicked person from among you so that you can stay pure....Don't even eat with such people.

> It isn't my responsibility to judge outsiders, but it certainly is your responsibility to judge those inside the church who are sinning.... God will judge those on the outside; but as the Scriptures say, "You must remove the evil[-doer] from among you" (1 Corinthians 5:6–7, 11–13, NLT).

The *conduct* of corrective/restorative church discipline includes both purpose and process. The purpose is fourfold:

1. To encourage sinning members to repent, thus restoring their righteousness before the Lord
2. To open the door for reconciliation with the body
3. To warn other members against such sin
4. To uphold the purity and blameless testimony of the church

The process of church discipline must be communicated to the members of the congregation. It is extremely important that grievance and disciplinary procedures be clearly and explicitly stated in the bylaws. This provides for *informed consent* of all members to the church's discipline policies and protects against possible litigation. The policies should be in accordance with Matthew 18, with the caveat that *exceptions to the first three steps may have to be made*.[1]

- Loving confrontation, in private
- Confrontation with two or three witnesses
- Confrontation before the congregation
- Termination of membership

Each succeeding step in the disciplinary process is contingent upon repentance. Step number four is in play only when repentance does not occur at any of the previous steps.

Termination of membership is not the end, but the beginning of the healing process for those who will not repent. It is also the beginning of the healing process for those who have continued in obedience to Christ and remained the faithful core of the church. I need to be very clear about this. We all have to face our sin: *individual sin*—being divisive and sowing discord; *corporate sin*—tolerating it. John White and Ken Blue are pretty direct in their exhortation to deal with our complicity in sinning.

> Not to deal with the matter [of sin] (or to procrastinate) is every bit as bad as to condone it. Both are sins. Condoning the sin represents rebellion against God and His Word.[2]

> Every single member in the church who is aware of the situation is sinning...in one way or another. The church is sinning by avoiding corrective church discipline.[3]

> Why is it that the thought of a holy and godly church concerns us so little?...We have become calloused to sin. To our great shame, *holiness* has become an empty word. Can it be because we have other goals for the church, goals which supersede her holiness?[4]

I remind you that termination of membership is not the end of our responsibilities. It's not, "Oh good, they're gone" or "Peace, at last!" We need to read and obey all of Matthew 18, specifically verse 18: "I tell you the truth, whatever you bind on earth has been bound in heaven, and whatever you loose on earth has been loosed in heaven."

Jesus' words about *binding and loosing*—removing from fellowship and receiving back into fellowship—are crucial for putting costly love into action for the healing of both those who are caught in the death grip of individual sin and those who are engaged in the corporate sin of tolerating it. We must be bold in our response to the hardhearted, unrepentant sin of our rebellious brothers and sisters. And we must fully understand that satanic powers will stand full-force against us to defeat us. But we must rest in the knowledge and assurance that we are entering into the spiritual battleground in the heavenlies, because what we bind and loose on earth is already bound and loosed in heaven. "Earth must confirm what heaven has already seen and judged."[5] We are aligning ourselves with Jesus and claiming the victory—already won—over sin.

Jesus is giving us real spiritual authority. He goes on in verses 19 and 20 to say, "Again, I tell you that if two of you on earth agree about anything you ask for, it will be done for you by my Father in heaven. For where two or three come together in my name, there am I with them." Jesus is still explaining binding and loosing. He is reinforcing both our authority to remove people from fellowship and to receive them back into fellowship when they repent of their sin. He is sealing the deal and inviting us to join Him and find peace where He is already at work building His kingdom.

Our actions on earth involve the powers of heaven, and with that in mind, we need to act not only with responsibility but also with great humility. We have no cause for being judgmental or feeling spiritually superior. Nor do we have any justification for taking pride in being tolerant of people who are sinning in ways that may be acceptable in our present-day culture. In addition to being corporate sin, tolerance of sin makes innocent people vulnerable to being manipulated into believing falsehoods without being motivated to check out the facts. Or, more subtly, they begin shifting how they see and feel about what's going on and curtailing their motivation to participate in the body life of the church.

What is an appropriate corrective response to sin? Not condemnation. Not arrogance. Not tolerance. Not indifference. Shouldn't we rather mourn? Paul thinks so: "You are proud *and* arrogant! And you ought rather to mourn...until the person who has done this (shameful) thing is removed from your fellowship *and* your midst!" (1 Corinthians 5:2, AMP). When a brother or sister in Christ falls into sin and falls away from fellowship, it is cause for weeping. That is where our heart needs to be as we enter into the process of binding and loosing.

In the corrective/restorative church discipline process, repentance leads to restoration of righteousness, which leads to *reconciliation*, which is the primary aim of binding and loosing. That is how we bring repentance back into play. The unrepentant sinner is removed from the church fellowship and given the opportunity to experience and reflect on his or her vulnerability to Satan's devices and schemes, without the protection and life-giving assurance and support provided by the fellowship of believers. Hopefully that will be a powerful inducement for repentance and return to Christian fellowship.

We must remember that reconciliation remains our ultimate goal, because God continues to love the sinner. We must too. Our first step is to mourn his or her hardhearted rebellion and removal from fellowship. Second, we must forgive and show love in whatever ways we can. This is where healing really begins. It restores us to righteousness from participation in the corporate sin of tolerating sin in our midst, and it heals our wounds from betrayal by longstanding friends. It is where we begin to look past the pain, shared with the many who have remained faithful and fruitful, from the barbaric destruction of relationships with the few who have participated in the savage defilement of the bride of Christ. And it is the beginning of the rehabilitation process that will hopefully bring those who willfully remain in rebellion back to righteousness and ultimately to reconciliation.

Forgiveness is the hinge for every door: peace, hope, and reconciliation. Oswald Chambers' distinctive Christian classic for more than seventy years, *My Utmost for His Highest*, tells us exactly why forgiveness opens those doors:

> If we are not heedful and pay attention to the way the Spirit of God works in us, we will become spiritual hypocrites. We see where other people are failing, and then we take our discernment and turn it into comments of ridicule and criticism, instead of turning it into intercession on their behalf.... Be careful that you don't become a hypocrite by spending all your time trying to get others right with God before you [humbly come before] Him yourself.[6]

Turn your ridicule and criticism into intercession on their behalf. That is Chambers' message for us today. If we do not, we are nothing more than spiritual hypocrites. Don't spend more time before the people for the Lord than before the Lord for the people! That is forgiveness.

I am talking about *unconditional forgiveness*. It looks like this:

- Do not wait for the offender to first repent.
- Pray for the Lord to forgive *and* bless the offender.

+ Be ready to reconcile.

Consider Jesus on the cross. The people at the foot of the cross did not seem to be one bit sorry. There was no repentance. None. In fact, in Mark 15:13–14 we read that they hurled insults at Him and shouted, "'Crucify him!'...[And] they shouted all the louder, 'Crucify him!'" And Jesus responded, "Father, forgive them"! (Luke 23:34). Note, too, that Moses did something similar when he was being besieged with complaints (see Numbers 14:19). Stephen, too, while his enemies threw stones at him, prayed seconds before his last breath, "Lord, do not hold this sin against them!" (Acts 7:60, NAS).

Oswald Chambers' call to intercessory prayer on their behalf, together with Jesus' example, are much more powerful than praying, "I forgive them." When we pray, *Father, forgive them*, we are in essence asking Him to release them from their guilt and to be merciful to them. And to bless them.

R. T. Kendall, in his best-selling book *Total Forgiveness*, gives it to us "pure and simple": "God did for us what we did not deserve. He therefore wants us to pass this on to others who don't deserve it."[7] Unconditional forgiveness is passing this on—praying for the Father to forgive them and bless them. This is not so much rejecting the sin as *bearing the sin* through intercession. It's not just about getting rid of the sin but even more importantly about redeeming the sinner. With continuing intercession on their behalf and showing unpretended love in whatever ways we can, given the unfortunate circumstances, the Holy Spirit can more freely work in their heart, away from conflict, and convict them to repent. And when they do repent, the repentant church can then joyfully join together in receiving them back into fellowship. In the meantime, "If it is possible, so far as it depends on you, live at peace with everyone" (Romans 12:18).

Consultation

Let's take a brief interlude right here. At this point, everything may look too complicated. Perhaps you long for the safety of simplicity over the danger of complexity. Maybe it seems too scripted, like A through Z guidelines for church conflict resolution. There may be a number of hesitations as well. Like some of these:

- Maybe you fear for the church's reputation in the community if conflict is made public.
- Perhaps you are too hesitant to confront friends with their sin or to believe that people you love could possibly want to do anything that might hurt you.
- Are you in denial that there is a growing conflict in the church, hoping it will resolve itself over time?
- Do you find it comforting to take refuge in the everyday ministries and other aspects of "normal" body life in order to hold on to an optimistic perspective on the health of the church, rather than face the gut-wrenching reality of the unhealthy conflict that exists below the surface?
- Does your personal response style to conflict—passive, evasive, defensive, or aggressive—keep you from an appropriate corrective response to sin?[8]
- Are you interpreting the parable of the wheat and the tares (see Matthew 13:24–30, 36–43) as prohibiting all attempts to separate the righteous and the rebellious, allowing openly contentious persons

to remain without repentance in the visible church? This is in opposition to the context that Jesus gives us that the field in which the two crops are growing is the world—not the church—so they must be allowed to grow together until the harvest at the end of the age (vv. 38–40). It also contradicts the apostolic injunctions such as 1 Corinthians 5 and Jesus' own words in Matthew 18.

It might be that you have a mistaken presumption that if you are spiritually mature you can just absorb the offense and forgive without bothering the sinner(s) or the church.

Do you believe that if you concentrate more on maturing the congregation through knowledge of Scripture, that will take care of it?

Are you marginalizing the importance of church discipline by your tacit approval of blatant justifications for intentionally rebellious behavior (e.g. "It's no big deal. Everybody has broken the covenant" of membership)?

Do you fear that things might become even more intolerable and get out of hand if you implement church discipline, leading to losing members and/or giving and ultimately to a church split?

John Howard Yoder, author of the classic *The Politics of Jesus*, addresses the irresponsibility of tolerating the intolerable in his essay *Binding and Loosing*:

> The real tragedy is...that as *church* we have come to respect...the willingness to live with directionlessness and with unreconciled divisions and conflicts.... We make a virtue of the "acceptance" of intolerable situations.... We have come to "live

with" a situation in which...we are satisfied with trying to do a decent job day by day without taking responsibility for the direction in which [our] churches...are evolving. A sense of not knowing where to turn next is pervasive.[9]

Not knowing where to turn next is almost always a large part of the problem in intolerable church conflict situations. Your own hesitance in the employment of church discipline may be causing you a great deal of grief, even panic, and you are desperate for some help. Perhaps you have already turned to a friend, a colleague, or your denomination for guidance. Maybe you have searched the Internet for counsel and have come to the conclusion that you need professional consultation.

My caution is this: Be very, very careful. Hiring a consultant can be hazardous to your health. I am reminded of my mom lying in a hospital bed on twenty-four-hour dialysis, dying. My brother and I were standing at the head of her bed, holding her hands and stroking her forehead. After a while, my brother went out to the nurses' station and checked Mom's chart. He was shocked to see that she was on twenty-one different medications! As we reviewed this new information and discussed it with the medical staff, I came to the horrifying conclusion that the medicine was killing the patient.

I have had some personal exposure to a Christian consulting group "killing the patient." I found them unsatisfactory in meeting professional standards for data collection and analysis, biblical standards for recommendations for seeking the kingdom of God and His righteousness, and personal standards for fairness and respect. That being said, I will cite some of my personal and professional observations—several of which attest to the testimonies of people in other churches as well—that could have general application in other conflict consultation situations.

First, appealing to an outside authority may very well be an evasion of one's own responsibility in following clear biblical guidelines. It can also be an evasion of working through intolerable personal feelings to completion—reconciliation—by choosing a consultant one hopes will more likely than not force the other side to submit.

Second, consultants are not usually committed personally to anyone in particular or to the organization. Therefore they can come in, do a quick survey, interview some people, do some analysis, make some recommendations, collect a fee, and are gone. And worst-case scenario, everyone is stuck with disappointing results and a large bill to pay. This sort of process can remove all hope and make matters much worse.

My third observation concerns some important *red flags*. Does the consulting group (or individual) have a conceptual framework that includes a one-size-fits-all theory of a "universal reality" of what every conflict supposedly looks like and what every church supposedly should look like? I find that presumptuous and naïve, in view of the wide variety of relevant levels of analysis of church conflict and the absence of a clear biblical picture of cookie-cutter churches. Does the consultant put his theories to the test with a deductive process of inquiry (theory-guided) posing as an inductive process of inquiry (participant-generated)? In other words, does he listen for descriptions of the participants' actual lived experience or just to their responses to his own preconceived ideas?

In short, does the consultant seek out how both God and Satan are at work in each particular church's conflict situation? Does he consider the uniqueness of the leading of the Holy

Spirit in forming each individual church in accordance with God's purposes for that church? Or does he do what he always does and find what he always finds?

This brings us to a fourth observation: Some consultants see themselves as *change agents* rather than facilitators. Armed with a theory of what every conflict looks like and a theory of what every church should look like, and doing what they always do and finding what they always find, they have an agenda. That agenda is not to resolve conflict but to actually use conflict as a catalyst to produce organizational change. This is not change based on the pre-condition of righteousness being re-established in the organization. First and foremost, understand that serious sin must be dealt with before instituting major changes. God will not fully bless churches that ignore this fundamental truth. Righteousness first, then restructuring.

The modus operandi for these consultants is very consistent with postmodern thinking. They seem to use their pre-established agenda to manipulate dissatisfaction and to provide for an extended period of time for restructuring the church to fit their self-proclaimed mold for *the* biblical church:

+ Seminar: stir up dissatisfaction with "old" ways of doing church.
+ Interviews and forums: escalate dissatisfaction with anxiety-provoking questions.
+ Report: arrive at crisis-invoking conclusions and recommendations.
+ Discovery process: prolong conflict to use as motivation for submitting to a collective change process of public confession, re-education regarding the

church as a community, and facilitated consensus for changing corporate values and vision and for structural/systemic changes as needed.

The "collective change process of public confession" is grounded on *brokenness*, which is a unifying principle of postmodernism. Brokenness is also a biblical concept, and is seen by these consultants as *the* biblical way for redeeming conflict. But in practice it often amounts to an unhealthy fixation on the act of being broken, an example of the end justifying the means.

I am reminded of Job 33:23–33, where Elihu explains how blessings can result from suffering and how Job should be restored to righteous living through confession of specific sin. Elihu is correct, but does his presumption of specific sin justify Job's loss of integrity by confessing to something that is not the fundamental issue? Is it really God who is behind a manufactured confession? This is the problem I see in the postmodern prescription of corporate confession—manipulating everyone to confess some specific sin in a public event to prove the existence of the shared experience of brokenness as an expression of building community.

True brokenness, however, is not limited to a public event. Rather, it is *a Holy Spirit-led confrontation of who God is and who we are not*, whether it is through unmanipulated corporate confession or the enduring process of daily dying to self. True brokenness is about *obedience* and *humility*. It is not a premeditated, presumptuous technique for manufacturing confession and promoting community.

The discovery process is accompanied by a postmodern approach to discerning truth. The best way to understand the Bible, it is argued, is through collective pooling of everyone's thoughts to shape a group consensus concerning the meaning of a given biblical text. It apparently only has meaning in the way it is relevant to the present context, as the group sees it. The effect of such a procedure, sad to say, is to shift the conversation from, "The Bible says..." to "I believe..." and from "I know..." to "I think..." or, "I feel...." This is a huge deviation from absolute, non-negotiable truth to a collective discovery process of interpretive consensus.

The danger, as I see it, is the devaluing of the objectivity of biblical truth. It is the promoting of the idea that we cannot know with certainty that what we read as individuals in the Bible is absolute truth—just as it is stated in the text. I believe we must acquire the factual knowledge in Scripture as God gave it. We must know Him as He wants to be known.

The wonderful thing about knowing God as He wants to be known is that He provides not just information but insight and personal transformation. We do not need group consensus per se. We need the Holy Spirit's guidance. It is He who will increase our delight in God's marvelous attributes, His character and purpose for our lives. It is He who will enable us to love the Lord with all our mind and strength, heart, and soul; to seek first His kingdom and His righteousness; to remember who He is and what He has done and will do. It is He who will arouse in us the passion to glorify God and enjoy Him forever.[10]

Finally, my fifth observation concerns a major part of the consultation process: the collection and presentation of evidence. This is where the most serious problems in the entire process occur. In order to decide on the quality of the conclusions, we must validate the quality of the evidence. In conflict situations, we are dealing with complaints, which need to be contextualized and properly understood. Judgments concerning the quality of complaints should not be based on just counting the complaints. We need to understand what the numbers mean. It is true that even healthy corporate systems (structures—forms and methods of organization—and patterns of thinking and acting) have flaws. But they are not fatal flaws based on the number of complaints.

Evidence derived from raw, count data is merely *suggestive evidence*. Numbers can mean anything and cannot be called conclusive evidence unless it is shown that the data collection process was valid. Even if a consultant adds more suggestive evidence to the suggestive evidence he already has, he still does not have conclusive evidence. That means we cannot accept the consultant's conclusions with a sufficient degree of confidence that they are true.

We should look first at how interviews are conducted, then how the data are presented. For example, are individual interviews standardized so that every person interviewed is asked the same questions, or are some questions sometimes just left out or rushed because of lack of time? Are group interviews conducted the same, or can one or more of them be dominated by a vociferous few so that some do not express themselves? Added to that, are the individual and group interviews interpreted in such a way that a few large/extended families can pile up the number of complaints? Families usually are in agreement with one another with their complaints (especially in a time of crisis, which brings them together in a common cause to distract them from their own ongoing problems), and if two families account for twenty members of a congregation of fifty, that really skews the data.

In the presentation of the results (e.g. illustrative tables and interpretive text), is information provided concerning what interviewees thought they were responding to—whom they were actually thinking of and over what period of time? Are categories of and statements about congregational life that are rated—e.g. leadership, caring for one another, "I believe this is a healthy church"—defined as to their meaning? Is information provided regarding how they were actually interpreted by the raters? Or, do the numbers merely indicate that there are varying degrees of opinion? You already know that!

Most importantly, are the facts regarding those varying opinions checked out? Or, is every complaint accepted with equal value regardless of age, regularity of attendance, recency of attendance, and membership status? If so, all you know for sure is something about the intensity of the conflict and nothing about the truth of the conflict!

Also, concerning the presentation of the results, Dr. David Zarefsky, a distinguished professor of communication studies, points out in his book *Argumentation*, many of the factors that can bias the evaluation of evidence. For example, two highly probable ways that judgments about the quality of evidence that supports the presenter's claims are affected are prior agreement with those claims and the presenter's enthusiasm for the content of his presentation and the dynamism of his delivery (energetic, winsome demeanor; attractive, engaging written reports; and/or video display).[11]

A footnote to the problematic reliance on suggestive evidence is the potential for deceptiveness of such evidence. Faulty, inconclusive evidence that is used to defend a particular conclusion is a handy vehicle for a particular kind of dishonesty. It is not usually an outright lie but often contains within it a complex web of unverified "facts." The fundamental dishonesty is the claim that the conclusion derived from the evidence at hand truly does matter. The truth of the matter, however, is that based on faulty evidence, this particular conclusion is both invalid and irrelevant.

6

Recovering from Conflict

How do we stay sane in these insane circumstances of unhealthy church conflict? In previous chapters we have investigated the nature of conflict as it may apply in your particular situation and examined in great detail the characteristics of troublemakers who cause division in the body of Christ. To refresh your memory, characteristics of those who cause division have been summarized by Rediger in his book *Clergy Killers*. He lists five that are particularly instructive—destructive, determined, deceitful, masters of disguise, and demonic—and describes them as follows:

- Clergy killers are marked by intentional destructiveness. They don't just disagree or criticize, they insist on inflicting pain and damaging their targets. Their tactics include sabotage [and] subverting worthy [ministries]. They are willing to violate the rules of decorum and caring that the rest of us try to follow...[and to] use tactics that we forbid ourselves to use.

- Clergy killers don't stop. They may pause, go underground, or change tactics, but they will intimidate, network, and break any rules of decency to accomplish their [agenda]. They insist that their agenda has priority.... They use bluster [and] threats...to appear...unstoppable.

- Clergy killers manipulate, camouflage, misrepresent, and accuse others of their own tactics. Their statements and negotiations are not trustworthy.

- They can present themselves as pious, active church members who are "only doing this for the good of the church." Often they convince naïve parishioners that they are raising legitimate issues. It is not uncommon for clergy killers to hide among their "allies of opportunity"—inciting [them] to do their dirty work for them.

- Spiritual leaders become symbols and scapegoats for the internal pain and confusion [clergy killers] feel [from their family histories and personal pathologies, which have become strongholds for demonic influence. [Unfortunately]...the mainline church and popular culture essentially have discarded the concept of evil by labeling sin and evil as mental illness or human failure.[1]

Now, in the midst of resolving the conflict, it is time to solidify your faith that has been strengthening and sustaining you through destructive, demonic conflict. It is time to pause and remember Jesus, who in the words of this timeless refrain is our Shelter in the time of storm: "The Lord's our Rock; in Him we hide, a Shelter in the time of storm; secure whatever ill betide, a Shelter in the time of storm." *It is time to begin recovery.*

Contemplation

"Be still and know that I am God" (Psalm 46:10). We begin the recovery process not by resisting but by resting. Not by fighting the trauma of the conflict but by resting in the Lord, prayerfully contemplating His Word. Contemplation is the first step in transitioning from combat to recovery.

Alone with God. This is where the real battle is joined. We find right away that we are not alone. When we begin to enter into our solitude, all those disruptive thoughts and feelings come crowding in, screaming for attention. Henri Nouwen in *With Open Hands* and *The Way of the Heart* describes it in exquisite detail:

> Everything returns: the bitterness, the hate, the jealousy, the disappointment, and the desire for revenge. But these [thoughts and] feelings are not just there; you clutch them in your hands as if they were treasures you didn't want to part with. You sit rummaging in all that old sourness as if you can't do without it, as if in giving it up, you would lose your very self.[2]

> As soon as I decide to stay in my solitude, confusing ideas, disturbing images, wild fantasies, and weird associations jump about in my mind like monkeys in a banana tree. Anger and greed begin to show their ugly faces. I give long, hostile speeches to my enemies.... Thus I try again to...restore my false self in all its vainglory. The task is to persevere...until all my seductive visitors get tired of pounding on my door and leave me alone.[3]

The task of contemplation is to persevere in hearing God's voice through Scripture reading and prayer throughout the recovery process, until your seductive visitors leave you alone and you regain your true identity in Christ.

Listen and yield

"Those who live in the shelter of the Most High will find rest in the shadow of the Almighty. This I declare of the Lord: He alone is my refuge, my place of safety; he is my God, and I am trusting him" (Psalm 91:1–2, NLT).

Trust and obey

> We can rejoice…when we run into problems and trials for we know that they are good for us—they help us learn to be patient. And patience develops strength of character in us and helps us trust God more each time we use it until finally our hope and faith are strong and steady. Then, when that happens, we are able to hold our heads high no matter what happens and know that all is well, for we know how dearly God loves us, and we feel this warm love everywhere within us because God has given us the Holy Spirit to fill our hearts with his love.
> —ROMANS 5:3–5, TLB

These are examples of Scripture passages from both the Old and New Testament that the Holy Spirit can use as a foundation for the recovery process. There are numerous others. There are also countless passages to build on the solid foundation. As you meditate on these you will discover the path you should take, and you will find peace. For example:

- Because suffering for Christ is our calling, it can also become an occasion for joy; therefore take joy in the privilege of actually participating in the sufferings of Christ (1 Peter 2:20–21; 4:13).

- Because the sufferings of Christ did not include the sufferings necessary on behalf of the church, we now have the privilege of suffering for the sake of the spiritual growth and health of the church, thereby sharing and fulfilling the sufferings of Christ (Colossians 1:24–29).

- As partners with Christ in His suffering we will share His glory when it is displayed to all the world—therefore endure insults and ridicule with self-control; serve with humility; continue to do good; and praise the Lord! (1 Peter 4:12–5:11).

- Live in peace—be a man of peace—and the God of love and peace will be with you (1 Corinthians 13:11).

Staying in your solitude and meditating on being a *man of peace*—as described in Scripture—would be of great benefit in your effort to remain sane in the insane circumstances in church conflict. Here is some of what you might find:

- Peace and blessedness rest upon the man of peace (Luke 10:5–6).

- He will be kept in perfect peace because his thoughts are fixed on the Lord (Isaiah 26:3).

- He is a maker and maintainer of peace and a searcher for peace (Matthew 5:9; 1 Peter 3:10–11; James 3:18).

- He lives at peace with everyone and is anxious about nothing (Romans 12:18; 1 Corinthians 13:11; Philippians 4:4–7).

- He is not quarrelsome or resentful, but kind and mild-tempered—preserving the bond of peace—and willing to suffer wrong (2 Timothy 2:24).

- He corrects his opponents with gentleness in the hope they will repent and escape the snare of the devil, who has held them captive (2 Timothy 2:25–26).

- He is blameless and upright and does not repay evil with evil (Psalm 37:37; Romans 12:17).

- His wisdom is from above, and righteousness is his fruit (James 3:17–18).

Obviously there are many Christian resources that are consistent with Scripture and are worthy of contemplative focus while alone with God. These words of advice by Francis Frangipane are a good example:[4]

"Satan's first weapon always involves luring our eyes from Christ."

"For you to succeed in warfare, your self-preservation instincts must be submitted to the Lord Jesus; for Christ alone is your true advocate."

"To humble yourself is to refuse to defend your image.... The strength of humility is that it builds a spiritual defense around your soul, prohibiting strife, competition and many of life's irritations from stealing your peace."

"Satan will not continue to assault you if the circumstances he designed to destroy you are now working to perfect you!"

"Our victory never comes from our emotions or our intellect. Our victory comes by refusing to judge by what our eyes see or our ears hear, and by trusting that what God has promised will come to pass."

"There is a tension underlying false discernment, an anxiety that pressures the mind to make a judgment. True discernment emerges out of a tranquil and pure heart, one that is almost surprised by the wisdom and grace in the voice of God."[4]

Confession

Being alone with God is like being in a furnace—a place of dwelling in God's healing presence as He locks us in and saturates us with the Holy Spirit. With the Holy Spirit's guidance, we are brought face-to-face with the parts of our unsanctified self that He selects for us to die to. He selects only those parts that will most perfectly transform us. But while He will not allow us to choose for ourselves what would undoubtedly be most comfortable and safe to throw into the fire, He will not allow the fire to consume us. He only does what is best for us. He "fits the furnace to our frame."

I learned about being alone with God in a furnace that fits our frame from a marvelous little book written by Dr. George Watson more than 100 years ago, titled *Soul Food*:

> The One who loves us best fits the furnace to our frame, and never once duplicates the pattern for any other soul. There are innumerable degrees of

suffering among God's chosen ones, yet in each case it is unique and personal. The ingredients of suffering are of infinite variety in kind and mixture, but the end to be accomplished is the same. God will not allow us to pick our crosses, or to exchange them with our neighbor....

The Lord selects for each of us those crucifixions which will most perfectly mortify us.... The very best and most fruitful of our mortifications are those in which God locks us in alone with Himself, and thereby saturates us with the Holy Spirit....

[When] God...hems us in alone with Himself, and deals with us and reveals His will to us...the closer we enter into union with Him, the more directly and exclusively He guides by His spirit.[5]

What is your degree of suffering in your present conflict? What are the personal ingredients of your suffering that are making a bad situation worse? What do you need to mortify in yourself to make the situation better? What do you think God has in mind?

What has God selected for you to die to? Pray David's prayer: "You hem me in—behind and before; you have laid your hand upon me....Search me, O God, and know my heart; test me and know my anxious thoughts. See if there is any offensive way in me, and lead me in the way everlasting" (Psalm 139:5, 23–24).

As you are alone with God, hemmed in with His hand upon you, and He lays bare your offensive ways, yield to the Holy Spirit as He guides you in the way of life and peace. Let Him speak to you through Scripture (following are some examples to get you started) as you prayerfully examine your unsanctified thought and behavior patterns that are not yet yielded to the Spirit. Let Him guide you and transform you as you confess your sins and ask for the Lord's forgiveness. Are you:

Abusive of your authority? "Am I dishonorably motivated and domineering?" (1 Peter 5:2–3)

Angry? "Do I stir up dissension, and am I hot-tempered?" (Proverbs 29:22)

Bitter? "Do I quarrel and slander?" (Ephesians 4:31)

Judgmental? "Do I presume evil intentions in others and speak critically with intent to hurt?" (Luke 6:37)

Lustful? "Do I crave sensual gratification of the flesh and harbor greedy longings of the mind?" (1 John 2:16)

Prideful? "Am I selfishly ambitious and arrogant?" (Philippians 2:3)

Untrustworthy? "Do I double-deal and distort the truth?" (Ephesians 4:25)

Unwilling to forgive? "Do I lack compassion for others and hold on to grievances?" (Colossians 3:13)

> *Unwilling to reconcile?* "Do I give in to revenge and give up on God?" (Romans 12:18)
>
> *Vengeful?* "Do I carry grudges and cause trouble that contaminates others?" (Hebrews 12:15)

You may need to confess to others in accordance with Matthew 5:22–24 because of something you have said or done against them. But be careful. There are some Christian speakers and authors who are saying that all sin affects the body of Christ and therefore must be confessed publicly, to the church. Biblically, that is not a requirement. If the sin was committed publicly, usually it would be appropriate to confess it publicly to those who were present. Or, if it was a grievous sin—especially by a person in leadership—of a moral or legal nature, it certainly could in most cases be confessed to the entire church. But if it was a private sin, it most certainly must be confessed to the Lord, who will tolerate no sin—public or private. And that would be sufficient.

Conciliation

First, alone with God, you faced the Lord. Then, through confession, you faced yourself. Now you must face your adversaries.

At some level, there is anger. Anger devours the angry. It does not, in and of itself, cause constructive change. If it sinks to the level of bitterness, it can kill the vitality of your soul. It can darken your mood, dampen your enthusiasm, destroy your joy, and defeat your hope in the Lord.

Conflict and anger are part of life and God can use them, but the dark night of the soul is not His desire for followers of Jesus. Anyone coming out of conflict is going to have some residual anger, so it must be dealt with. It does no good to deny your unresolved anger, displace it onto someone or something that is "safe," or discharge it with a cathartic outburst to "put it behind us" or to "get over it."

Common knowledge says that we must get rid of the bad and replace it with something good. As simple as that sounds, it works. Recovery from habitual, destructive thoughts and behaviors demands that we stop the bad (and there are tools to do that) and replace it with something good. We definitely should not leave a void for another destructive habit to come in and mess up our life. When spiritual warfare is involved, deliverance from demonic influence must also be followed up with the counteracting presence and influence of the Holy Spirit.

Biblically, you can get rid of your anger with confession and *unconditional forgiveness*. This is the fundamental requirement for both mental health and spiritual well-being. By now, hopefully, you have confessed the log in your own eye. If so, you are ready to replace it with something good—unconditional forgiveness of your adversaries. Perhaps you have already done that as well, as presented in the previous chapter.

Don't be a spiritual hypocrite by spending more time before your adversaries trying to get them right with the Lord, than before the Lord interceding on their behalf, asking Him to forgive them and to bless them.

Don't wait for them to first repent. Show them unpretended love in whatever ways you can. Be ready to reconcile.

You will know you have recovered from the conflict when you have forgiven (and perhaps even been forgiven) and replaced your anger with the *conciliatory attitude* of unpretended love and readiness to reconcile. And you will know, when unhealthy conflict inflicts itself on you again, what will happen when you confess your own sin and forgive it in others. Cornelius Plantinga has expressed it beautifully in his article *Rehearsing Forgiveness*:

> Christians [break the cycle of sin] by undertaking to confess and forgive it.... Each time we [confess] we put out a contract on our old self—the timidly self-righteous self or the proud grudge-bearing self—and then pull the trigger ourselves. Each time we forgive we absorb evil without passing it on, and then rise, like Christ, with healing in our wings.[6]

A conciliatory attitude is probably expressed best for both leaders and followers in terms of love, drawing on 1 Corinthians 13:4–7:

> Love is patient and has good manners.
>
> Love is not jealous, boastful or proud.
>
> Love is not rude and does not demand its own way.
>
> Love is not irritable and does not fly off the handle (or nurse resentment).
>
> Love is not quick to take offense (but lays aside all recriminations and talking about others behind their backs) and keeps no record of when it has been wronged.
>
> Love does not approve of evil but delights in the truth.

> Love is always ready (to forgive,) to trust, to hope, and to endure through every circumstance.

I believe that biblically, *good followership* is just as important as good leadership. Members of the congregation are to be Christlike followers. Unfortunately, followers come in three flavors: the good, the bad, and the ugly.

The good

> Leaders not only need the Holy Spirit's faithfulness but also the Spirit's faithfulness *mediated by the body of Christ.*
>
> We must not view them as we view public figures, targets for the venomous darts of our criticism. They are our fellow believers. We must build walls of prayer around them. But we must do more. They need overt expressions of our concern. And as we give them, we shall begin to see there are two sides to the coin of accountability, leaders' accountability to God for our spiritual welfare and our accountability to God to be faithful to those leaders who stand in need of our fidelity.[7]

The bad

> A denominational executive once came to our church to observe some of our meetings. He later commented to me: "These fellows (the antagonists) are really powerful people, aren't they? Their personalities seem to overwhelm the others, intimidate them, leave them speechless. It is

obvious to me that they are intensely angry about something deeply rooted in their past....[But] *no one is resisting them. The silent majority [the followers] are leaving you standing alone*" (italics added).[8]

The ugly

> A deacon chairman tells of being accosted by an irate church member in the halls of the church. "She stuck her finger in my face and said, 'If you can't straighten out that preacher then we will just have to do it for you.' She wasn't just talking. She was screaming at the top of her voice. Her face was red and the veins in her forehead were protruding so much I thought they would burst."[9]

Dr. Guy Greenfield in his book *The Wounded Minister* raises a very interesting question concerning poor followership: "Why is it that when a minister is under attack by an antagonist or a small group of 'uglies,' some of those who are usually friends and supporters become thunderously silent, meek, and mild, and passively allow the attacks to continue unabated?"[10] Why are they just like the rest of the "silent majority" who fail to stand up and challenge the false accusations and half-truth innuendoes? This, I would dare say, is one of the craziest aspects of the insane circumstances in church conflict. It is also one of the most painful disappointments for a wounded minister to endure. Good followers are good friends who are faithful to those leaders who stand in need of their fidelity.

That being said, we must remember that the ultimate resolution of church conflict is reconciliation. You can have complete recovery from the conflict but still not have complete resolution of the conflict. It is important to realize that. You may or may not be reconciled with your adversaries.

Some people will say to you, "You haven't forgiven them because you haven't reconciled with them." That is unfair, and it is untrue. To forgive does not mean entering back into an abusive relationship to, in all probability, be abused again. Nor does it imply that fellowship will be restored "just like it used to be." Some things can never be the same again. Nor can we just "forgive and forget." Evil leaves an imprint on our emotional memory. Our job is to forgive unconditionally with intercessory prayer and a conciliatory attitude of unpretended love and readiness to reconcile when repentance is forthcoming.

In the meantime, Paul has given us crystal-clear marching orders in Romans 12:18–21.

> If it is possible, as far as it depends on you, live at peace with everyone. Do not take revenge, my friends, but leave room for God's wrath, for it is written: "It is mine to avenge; I will repay," says the Lord. On the contrary: "If your enemy is hungry, feed him; if he is thirsty, give him something to drink. In doing this, you will heap burning coals [of blessing] on his head." Do not be overcome by evil, but overcome evil with good.

By now your recovery process should be in full swing. It's time to address anger again, in a new light. Earlier we talked about getting rid of your unresolved anger by confessing the log in your own eye. That was self-righteous anger, or self-righteous indignation: raw emotion, coupled with distorted thoughts, connected with feeling personally violated and taking offense.

As the Holy Spirit guides you through the recovery process, He fills your heart with desire for the Father to forgive and bless those who have wronged you. And He enables you to show love to them in whatever ways you can and live at peace with them if it is possible, as far as it depends on you. He also enables you to replace your self-righteous indignation with holy anger at anything that profanes the name of the Lord or defiles His bride. That is called *righteous indignation*.

You've gone through a very troublesome time. You've been tormented by the inexcusable but not unforgivable slandering of personal reputations and defiling of corporate gatherings. You've been on the road to recovery. Now let the Holy Spirit speak to you: "When the enemy shall come in like a flood, the Spirit of the Lord will lift up a standard against him *and* put him to flight" (Isaiah 59:19, AMP). The standard He has for you, at such a time as this, is righteousness. The Holy Spirit is raising up the standard of righteous indignation within you and convicting the slanderers and the defilers for you. David's exhortation is to the point: "Be agitated [angry], but do not sin; commune in your heart upon your bed, and be still. Offer sacrifices of righteousness, and put your trust in the Lord" (Psalm 4:4–5, BERKELEY).

In the previous chapter, Paul's laundry list of things to be righteously indignant about and his advice on how to respond to them are good examples of how to apply the standard of righteousness. However, they have a precondition: dying to all self-righteous indignation. It is imperative that we focus entirely on the righteousness of God, not on the righteousness of ourselves! Following is where this fits in the overall process of resolving rebellious church conflict:

> *Unconditional forgiveness*—intercessory prayer and a conciliatory attitude of unpretended love and readiness to reconcile. Precondition: Repent—get the log out of your own eye.
>
> *Righteous indignation*—holy anger at anything that profanes the Lord's name or defiles His bride. Precondition: Die to self-righteous indignation—focus your thoughts on the righteousness of God rather than the righteousness of yourself.
>
> *Righteous reconciliation*—receiving back into fellowship those who have repented, thereby restoring the purity of the church. Precondition: Live at peace with those who have profaned the Lord's name or defiled the church if it is possible, as far as it depends on you.

There is no time limit for this peacemaking process. It is never too late for reconciliation. We must keep on showing God's love—centering our thoughts on Jesus, walking in the path of righteousness for His name's sake, and living with our hearts filled with His presence. And, as it was prophesied long ago, "This One will be *our* peace" (Micah 5:5, NAS).

Reframing the Future

As I catch my breath and collect my thoughts at this juncture, I have a sense of peace and calm, like after a storm. Everything is clear, while during a raging storm things can get pretty clouded, vague, and confused.

Confusion seems to be different from conflict per se. Conflict is more about controversial, nontrivial issues, where opposing claims are made and evidence is presented to support the claims through argumentation. Confusion, on the other hand, is more about contentious, quarrelsome personal feelings, where the person being impugned has no argument to make because of the vagueness about what is wrong and the shakiness of what can be done about it. Conflict is about decision-making. Confusion is about crazy-making.

The burden of this book is facing down the curse of unhealthy conflict, where well-meaning argumentation is replaced by antagonistic competition. Unhealthy conflict is loaded with confusion, creating numerous demonstrations of division and disorder, such as the following:

+ Dissension through deception and secrecy
+ Erosion of relationships
+ Perversion of normal practices

- Regression from rational adult discourse to irrational childish outbursts

Confusion is like a foreboding fog that settles down over God's people, obscuring their vision and subduing their passion. It's a pretty reliable indicator that Satan is the instigator when the bride's attacked. Confusion creates uncertainty in the thoughts and emotions of those who are being abused by the heartless acts of others: puzzlement, disappointment, and indecision. Where is this crazy-making stuff coming from? Why are previously trustworthy people suddenly being rebellious? How should we respond to a number of reasonable but seemingly contradictory biblical options?

For example, should we *avoid troublemakers* (see 2 Timothy 3:1–5), or should we *warn them* once and then a second time and after that have nothing to do with them (Titus 3:10)? Or should we flat out *remove them* from the congregation (see 1 Corinthians 5:6–13)? Or, any combination or all of the above? Confusion produces hesitation that can easily result in indecision. And the conflict within oneself can easily be greater than the conflict with the troublemakers!

We know from scripture that God is not a God of confusion but of peace (1 Corinthians 14:13). And we know that "wherever there is jealousy (envy) and contention (rivalry and selfish ambition), there will also be confusion (unrest, disharmony, rebellion) and all sorts of evil *and* vile practices" (James 3:16, AMP). Satan is the author of confusion and rebellion.

By now, hopefully, you can better understand your own situation. Was it (or is it) more about confusion than about conflict? Now do you see that Satan was (or has been) the enemy all along? Do you see your responses during the "conflict" in a different light? Can you now move forward differently since your adversaries were not (or are not) the enemy? If so, the confusion is over! You can sing a new song: "The LORD reigns.... The seas have lifted up, O LORD, the seas have lifted up their voice. [But You are] mightier than the noise of many waters.... Your [standards] stand firm, and holiness adorns your house, O LORD, for ever."[1]

As you look back, do you now see that you have no regrets about what you did and no thoughts about what "could have been?" If that is not the case, do you desire to do better so that you can finish well? If you were winding down your ministry in preparation for relocation or for retirement, did you finish well?

REDEEMING THE CONFLICT

Finishing well is, not surprisingly, a process of redeeming "conflict." It is not defined by the presence or absence of "conflict" or even the degree of "conflict." Finishing well, however, is always an issue of ends and means. We usually think about the ending point of a job or career as when we slow to a stop, pack up our stuff, take the pictures off the wall, turn in the keys, and turn off the lights. Then we ponder *what* we did, what we accomplished, what things we got done. That's the world's way. It's not Jesus' way.

Jesus' way is not what we accomplish along the way to wherever we're going. It's *how* we get there. It's who we are, not what we achieve, along the way. Are we obedient to Jesus' way in everything we are doing? Are we being faithful in following Him, all the way to the end? Or, are we adopting the very ways and means that Jesus Himself rejected? Is it about relevance, status, power, success, self-preservation—just feeding the conflict? Is it all about securing our importance in others' eyes and avoiding personal humiliation? Or is it, plain and simple, about Jesus—following Jesus?[2]

Finishing well is also a matter of vision. In the wise words of Dallas Willard in *The Great Omission*, to finish well is to "sustain the inner spiritual fire that keeps mission and ministry in its [sic] proper place, preventing them from becoming the limiting vision that obsesses us and eventually strangles us."[3] We must not put out the fire of God that resides within and replace it with, in Willard's words, pretending and being presumptuous about ourselves and pushing as if the outcome depends on us. We have no other God-appointed business than making disciples, without frustration, and in joyful, loving abandonment to God.

> The result is assurance that the mission and the ministry will be accomplished, in God's time and in God's way. They don't need to be the vision, and the goals we set for them are God's business, not ours. We do the very best we know, we work hard, and even self-sacrificially. But *we do not carry the load*, and *our ego is not involved* in any way with the mission and the ministry. In our love of Jesus and his Father, we truly have abandoned our life to him. Our life is not an object of deep concern.[4]

Finishing well is not a deep personal concern for a disciple of Jesus. Making disciples and living a life of loving abandonment to God is. Then, in God's time and in God's way, we will finish well. We will know, as Paul did when he was concluding his ministry: "I have fought the good fight, I have finished the race, I have kept the faith. Now there is in store for me the crown of righteousness, which the Lord, the righteous Judge, will award to me on that day—and not only to me, but also to all who have longed for his appearing" (2 Timothy 4:7–8).

Finishing well by submitting to Jesus' way—fighting the good fight, finishing the race and keeping the faith—redeems conflict by bringing the conflict under the lordship of Jesus Christ. That is the proper beginning for reframing the future:

- Redeeming the conflict
- Renewing your calling
- Returning to your first love

Renewing Your Calling

It is not uncommon to be ambivalent about having finished well. Intellectually yes, emotionally no. You're okay with your own actions but saddened by other people's actions. There's a vague feeling of not having made a difference in people's lives, emptiness in your own life, and apprehensiveness about the future. Nothing seems to have mattered in the past or seems to matter in the present, so why plan for the future? That's not really true, but it sure feels that way. It's like living in a vacuum—a space entirely empty of matter. Only this is an *existential vacuum*, an emotional space where nothing matters, where you feel that indeed you do not matter, that you no longer have a clear sense of identity.

It is imperative that you not allow all the awful things that happened in the past to frame how you perceive the future. To the contrary, what you seek for the future should determine what you recall from the past. If the future you choose to believe in is honoring to the Lord, the past you choose to remember will be honoring to Him too. This is a future that emerges in the present, which is the most significant period of time. It is when, where, and how God chooses to work. Join Him in what He is doing where you are now.

I am talking about the basis for one's calling to the church, which is contained in Jesus' words, "I am the Way, the Truth and the Life" (John 14:6). We have already seen Jesus as the Way—how we are to follow Him. Now we must picture Jesus as *the Life*—who we are in Him. It is in Jesus alone that we find our identity. This identity is transformational and brings us into community with others who embrace the same identity and with whom we gather as church.

The crucial point that needs to be made is that entrance into the community is the result of, not the means to, our identity in Christ. It is not the other way around (we find our identity in Christ by entering into the church community). The New Testament, in fact, confirms this. Truly entering into the community is possible only through possession of the Life:

> The one who existed from the beginning is the one we have heard and seen.... He is Jesus Christ, the Word of Life.... And now we testify and announce to you that he is the one who is eternal life.... We are telling you about what we ourselves have actually seen and heard, so that you may have fellowship with us. And our fellowship is with the Father and with his Son, Jesus Christ.
> —1 JOHN 1:1-3, NLT

"So that you may have fellowship with us"—this clearly positions community as a fruit of redemptive identity. If we have accepted Jesus through the Holy Spirit and therefore have the Life, we will be part of the church community.[5] However, we are warned by Richard Greene (referred to in chapter 3), a leading proponent of church multiplication through the Holy Spirit-driven transformed lives of disciples who make disciples who make disciples:

> When we begin with community, we run the danger of bypassing the requisite transformation the redemptive identity produces. John [in the above quote] is saying we are connected to God and to one another through this identity and our personal experience with Christ is the connecting point....
>
> The problem is our focus has been on the development of the community as a means of producing the transformation, and we have neglected the transformation.... [Supposedly] the community (church) is successful if it is big and getting bigger. [But] the bigger we become, the more challenging it becomes to ensure that true transformation is taking place.[6]

"Our personal experience with Christ is the connecting point" for fellowship with God and with one another. Therefore our calling as individuals and as a church is to choose Jesus the Life. That is also revealed to us in the Old Testament: "I have set before you life and death, blessings and curses. Now choose life, so that you and your children may live and that you may love the Lord your God, listen to his voice, and hold fast to him. For the Lord is your life" (Deuteronomy 30:19–20).

The calling the Lord has set before us—Jesus the Way and Jesus the Life—is a calling to transformational teaching and disciple-making. A calling to make disciples who make disciples—who love the Lord, listen to His voice, and hold fast to Him; a calling to a disciple-making church.

In Chapter 1, I reviewed the results of a three-year research project at Willow Creek Community Church. Willow Creek had been for over three decades the megachurch champion of the attractional, seeker-sensitive model. They had built their church around the assumption that if you provide programs to meet everyone's needs and as more people participate in them, the result will be more transformed lives. They assumed that the more involved people get in their church, the more they become like Christ. They were wrong. They now know that is not what was really happening.

A *disciple-making church* is not an attractional church. She is a missional church. The following highlights the differences:

Missional	Attractional
(Gather and Go)	(Come and See)
Is Holy Spirit-driven	Is program-driven
Focuses on what God is doing	Focuses on what people want
Feeds passion for Christ	Feeds consumer-oriented participation
Births disciples	Builds the church
Focuses on transformation: redeeming lives; making new lives	Focuses on transaction: repairing lives; making better lives
Focuses on transcendence: taking people beyond where they are; emphasizing the spiritual (Spirit-led) over the natural (man-led)	Focuses on relevance: keeping people where they are; emphasizing the natural (man-led) over the spiritual (Spirit-led)
Plants new churches as the result of fulfilling the Great Commission	Plants new churches as the means for fulfilling the Great Commission.[7]

John 3:6 is foundational for a disciple-making church: "Flesh gives birth to flesh, but the Spirit gives birth to spirit." Following Richard Greene's perspective, if a church is born out of a man-

led, program-driven vision, that's likely what she will always be. If a church is born out of a Spirit-led, passion-motivated vision, that's likely what she will always be. This is, or should be, a huge issue for church planters. If a new church desires to make disciples in obedience to the Great Commission, it would be wise to make every effort *to* make disciples *by* making disciples, right from the very beginning. It's all about DNA. How you start is what you become. It is almost impossible to "add the Spirit" to the DNA of a program-driven, consumer-oriented church later.

If a church is born out of a Spirit-led, passion-motivated vision, disciples have been transformed by the Holy Spirit and are making spiritually transformed disciples. They, in turn, are also making disciples, and as they continue to multiply, the opportunity often arises to gather together as a church. If so, they will begin with the end in mind: a low-cost daily pattern of disciples making disciples empowered by the transforming work of the Holy Spirit and passion for Jesus. Structures and ministries will be added as they are needed and can be supported and managed by their emerging church. This is *being church*. It is being a disciple-making church born of the Spirit, a holy living entity of disciples being harmoniously built together on the foundation of anointed biblical witnesses and framed together in Jesus for a habitation of the Holy Spirit (see Ephesians 2:19–22).

Contrast the disciple-making church with how churches are usually started. A group of Christians (more than likely, none of whom has made a disciple before) raise financial resources to rent or build a building and pay a pastor's salary, organize programs to meet the perceived needs of their target group, and do mass advertising of their launch date throughout the surrounding community. That's *doing church*. And we wonder why so many contemporary churches are so spiritually impoverished.

For existing churches that are just doing church and would prefer to be disciple-making churches, the transition will not be easy. There will need to be a radical refocusing of the vision for fulfilling the Great Commission and reformulation of the corporate core values, along the following lines:

- Return to the roots of biblical Christianity
- *Be fruitful* and multiply—the law of reproduction
- Be fruitful and *multiply*—the principle of multiplication
- Join what God is doing right now—the missional supremacy of the Great Commission
- Walk in the Spirit—give priority to spiritual transformation[8]

You have just been through difficult and painful conflict. This is a God-appointed time to renew your calling. Something needs to change. Just remember, as someone once wisely said, If we always do what we've always done, we'll always get what we've always gotten!

You don't need to change everything. Change does not need to be chaotic. Perhaps you've been through a time of overconcern regarding internal operations, with church maintenance more than with ministry. Maybe things got out of hand with political infighting for control of church governance. Now is the time to establish the missional supremacy of the Great Commission. Now is the time to cast the vision of disciples making disciples. Now is the time to join God in what *He* is doing *now*.

It is beyond the scope of this book to go into this in great detail, but it can be useful to do at least two more things. First, try to form a simple picture out of the complexity of all the pieces that don't seem to fit together anymore. Bill Hull (referred to in Chapter 1) presents a very clear overview of the full scope of ministry that a disciple-making church is trying to accomplish in the life of each disciple:

- Deliverance—salvation (saved by faith)
- Development—disciple-building (being established in the faith)
- Deployment—disciple-making (spreading the faith)[9]

The second thing that would help build a biblical base for change is recognizing an insidious, fundamental aspect of church conflict that will not change. It's another DNA issue that goes all the way back to Genesis and that is referred to allegorically by Paul in the book of Galatians.

I am referring to the story of conflict between Sarah and Hagar and between their sons, Isaac and Ishmael. In Genesis 16 we read that Sarah (Sarai), the wife of Abraham (Abram), has borne him no children. So she decides that her maidservant named Hagar can get the job done with Abram; and she does, giving birth to a son named Ishmael. In verse 12 we read that an angel of the Lord says to Hagar, "He will be a wild donkey of a man; his hand will be against everyone and everyone's hand against him, and he will live in hostility toward all his brothers." Earlier, Hagar's hand had been against Sarah, despising her and making her suffer, and Sarah had mistreated Hagar right back.

In Genesis 17:19–21, we read that Sarah will also give birth to a son and name him Isaac, and God says that He will establish an everlasting covenant for him and his descendants. But

God also says He will bless Ishmael and make him fruitful. His covenant blessing, however, is for Isaac. Finally, we jump to Genesis 21:1–10 and read about the birth of Isaac and that the enmity between Hagar and Sarah has expanded to Ishmael's maltreatment of Isaac.

That brings us to Galatians 4:21–31. Along with John 3:6, Galatians 4:31 is also foundational for a disciple-making church: "We are not children of the slave woman, but of the free woman." Again following Richard Greene's perspective, we are not children of the natural, but of the supernatural, which is allegorical or symbolic of how God works.

This passage from Galatians has three components: the people, the problem, and the promise. The people are Abraham, Sarah, Hagar, Isaac, and Ishmael. Abraham is the bearer of the seed. By making disciples we are passing on the seed of Abraham. We are fulfilling the promised blessing of all nations with God's redemptive purposes through Christ, through the seed of Abraham. We are planting the life of Christ, not launching institutions.

Sarah represents the Spirit and therefore God's work. A Spirit-filled, disciple-making church is from Sarah. Hagar, on the other hand, represents the flesh: self-effort. Hagar symbolizes the natural, institutionalized church system. She was not evil, just misguided. The big buildings, celebrity pastors, and profusion of programs are not bad, but they are birthed from the natural and must be subordinated by the glory of God, with Sarah as mother not Hagar. We must be children of the free woman, not of the slave woman!

Isaac is the son of promise. He was born by the power of the Spirit: the supernatural way. Ishmael is the son of bondage to the present religious system. He was born in the natural, fleshly way. God said He'd bless Ishmael and make him fruitful. He would not and will not, however, bless the Ishmael system with the promise, the covenant blessing. Paul is very clear about that: "[Christ] redeemed us in order that the blessing given to Abraham might come to the Gentiles through Christ Jesus, so that by faith we might receive the promise of the Spirit" (Galatians 3:14); "You, brothers, like Isaac, are children of the promise" (Galatians 4:28).

The problem is two-fold. First, we will always have Ishmael in the church. The *Ishmael presence* is the "insidious, fundamental aspect of church conflict that will not change," that I referred to earlier. Perhaps your recent conflict was resolved through church discipline or even a church split, but be prepared to face Ishmael again.

Second, Ishmael will always persecute Isaac. Because Ishmael is ever-present, he could avoid controversy for a long time. But the hostile *Ishmael attitude* is fertile ground for conflict—all the way from petty disagreement to full-blown rebellion. When you first recognize the Ishmael presence in your congregation, before serious conflict develops, you don't need to wait for full-blown rebellion to respond. The question is how to respond.

Understand up front that you cannot turn those with an Ishmael attitude into faithful children of the promise by discipling them. What you can do is be nonjudgmental and loving toward them and let them continue to attend and participate in church activities. But you will want to expend most of your time and energy with those who are living in the vision of multiplying disciples—those who are faithful children of the promise.

The promise is the redemption of the church, from the Ishmael rebellion to the *Isaac remnant*. Hagar must return to proper relationship with the Lord, as maid not mother. God in His goodness has promised to love and bless those who follow in the way of

Hagar, even if they are pruned away or split away from the faithful Isaac remnant and start their own church. However, a church born into bondage to the present religious system will not inherit the promise given to Abraham and passed on through Isaac and Christ Jesus. And if a church is born out of rebellion, without repentance, then the blessings will fall away as well.

For the faithful Isaac remnant, the greatest blessing is metaphorically entering into Sarah's tent and becoming the undefiled bride of Christ—as symbolized by the marriage of Isaac and Rebekah in Sarah's tent. (See Genesis 24:67.) Nothing is more important than restoration of the purity of the church in proper covenant relationship with the Lord![10]

8 Returning to Your First Love

THE GREATEST CHALLENGE for the wounded church will be to recover from the *collective grief* caused by those who chose to stay away and wait and see until things improved to their satisfaction, to intentionally break the covenant of membership, and to refuse to participate in the corporate observation of the sacraments of baptism and communion. This is not just about hurt feelings and personal attacks. Those things are direct attacks on the church herself. They defile the body of Christ—the bride of Christ! Therefore, they are to be met with Christ-like intolerance and righteous indignation (see chapters 5 and 6).

Collective grief weighs heavily on the spirit. Jesus said that in times of increasing lawlessness people's love of God will grow cold. (See Matthew 24:10–12.) Many will begin to emotionally and spiritually withdraw from the church. Tragically, as they just go through the motions, they will also withdraw from intimacy with God. They will forsake their first love.

The wounded church must return to her first love. The first step is to be *restored to holiness*, because the church is a habitation for the presence of a Holy God by His Spirit. I devoted chapters 4 and 5 to restoring church purity through church discipline. In the context of the present chapter, we need to understand that we dare not restrict holiness to some prescription for individual behavior or description of the reputation of a local church. Church discipline must not measure holiness apart from the God-initiated touch of the Holy One Himself. Holiness is given and defined by the presence and awesomeness of God. Thus we shout and sing, "Holy, holy, holy is the Lord God Almighty, who was, and is, and is to come" (Revelation 4:8).

Finding Peace

The wounded church must also be committed to finding peace. God's purpose in every conflict is to deepen our relationship with Jesus as we seek to find peace. His desire for us, stated in Jeremiah 29:11, is that we find peace and reaffirm our future and hope in Jesus. This is done most effectively by finding and following Jesus, the Way, the Truth, and the Life, in the conflict. I am again reminded of Job, when Elihu has ended his lengthy monologue and Job is granted his deeply longed-for dialogue with God: "Then the Lord answered Job out of the storm" (Job 38:1). God spoke from the storm. That is what finding peace is all about; Jesus speaking to us and walking with us in the midst of the conflict. Jesus is our Peace. Finding our Peace is more about redeeming conflict than resisting conflict (*keeping peace*) or resolving conflict (*making peace*).[1]

In Ephesians 2:14–18 we read that Jesus in *Himself* destroyed the barrier—the dividing wall of hostility—to make peace between Jews and Gentiles. He reconciled both sides of the conflict through the cross, thereby bringing their feud to an end. In Him, through the cross, both Jews and Gentiles gained access to the Father by one Spirit and found peace.

We can easily apply this powerful biblical example to the church in the twenty-first century. Jesus is our Peace (too). He is the author and the substance of our being at peace with God and in our encounters with one another. He has made peace in our conflict situations already, on the cross. So as we walk in the Jesus *Way* through whatever the conflict may be, with Jesus the *Life* in us, the Holy Spirit reveals the Peace already within us. He also gives us the strength and grace to obey all that Jesus commanded and lived out Himself, as we follow Him as His instruments for making peace. Our goal is being men (persons) of peace—*peace*—as described in Chapter 6.

Obviously, we cannot wait until the conflict is manageable before we begin our search for peace. Finding peace is finding Jesus in the midst of the conflict. We must start as soon as we recognize the presence of conflict and ratchet up our search during the worst of the conflict. True conflict resolution radiates out from the eye of the storm. It does not fight a hopeless fight to get through the storm on our own terms, blinded by our preconceived theories, to the green pastures and still waters of our own making. Jesus the *Truth* shines out from the midst of the darkest, stormiest of times and gives us peace. Not manufactured, pseudo-peace. Real peace.

Finding peace—finding Jesus—in the midst of church conflict is a process of turning away from the unseemly noise of division and the untoward loss of direction. It is a process of intentionally turning with Jesus in the direction of the green pastures and still waters that He provides. He is our Shepherd and we are the people of His pasture. He has already been leading us in the path of righteousness and through the valley of the shadow of death. We fear no evil, for He is with us! (See Psalms 23:1–4 and 95:7.) Righteousness first, and then peace.[2]

Finding Peace and choosing Life—that is returning to our first love: Jesus. He is the One who invites us to lie down in green pastures and leads us beside still waters. He is the One who revives our soul. And He is the One who proclaims, "Fear not, little flock, for the Father is pleased to give you the kingdom" (Luke 12:32). This is the ultimate direction our first love is taking us, from the church per se to the kingdom. No longer is the church's mission doing church work. Now it is doing kingdom work.

There is a threefold pattern in Jesus leading the way. First, Jesus *brings to us* the promise of the Holy Spirit to expose evil and guide us through the conflict and into the future. One way He can do that is through prophecy. Unfortunately, this can be a source of conflict in itself. When a prophecy is given for the church as a whole, some in the congregation may object that prophecy is not appropriate in this day and age, or they may be fearful that the content of the prophecy will harm the church. These people will not hear nor will they obey the prophecy. If they are also in rebellion, they will stay together, mired in their discontent, not joining the congregation in hearing the word from the Lord.

There is a very real possibility, however, of false prophecy. True, anointed prophecy meets several tests:

- It squares with Scripture.
- It conveys hope as well as warning.
- It is not arrogant and self-promoting.
- It is delivered with compassion, not contempt.
- It does not manipulate, intimidate, or attempt to control the life of the body.
- It bears witness to the character, purity, and fruit of the prophet's life.

Jack Deere in his book *The Beginner's Guide to the Gift of Prophecy* adds, "Faultfinding and anger are not the signs of a prophetic calling, but rather of a wounded heart that has refused God's healing mercy."[3] Fuchsia Pickett in *Presenting the Holy Spirit* clarifies Deere's point about corrective prophecy:

> The ministry of *corrective prophecy* belongs only to the leader of the flock or to another minister properly submitted to that pastoral leadership. A layperson should never attempt to correct, condemn, or chastise a congregation or an individual through the use of the gift of prophecy. According to the Scriptures, the simple gift of prophecy that operates apart from the office of a prophet is to be used for edification, comfort, and exhortation (1 Cor. 14:3). Correction of a church or believer corresponds to the office of the prophet, to one who is walking in a place of responsibility and accountability before God for a particular group of people. The purpose of prophecy, then, is first to exalt Jesus and then to build the Body of Christ.[4]

Anointed prophecy can be given by the Holy Spirit to provide a prophetic framework for conflict, from beginning to end, and for vision for the future. That is exactly what we experienced in a strong, healthy small church known for transformational teaching, prayer, giving, and caring for others. We had no clue that conflict was on the horizon and would soon come sweeping down upon us.

Then one day God spoke. He prepared us for what was to come: "You are going to experience something very devastating.

Every life will be touched by it. You will all be shaken. The Lord is going to sift the wheat from the chaff. You are all being tested. You need to stand firm and *stand together*" (italics added).

Four months later God spoke to us again. He mobilized us for the future:

My Church, My Gathering

> You are like a rose—strong, yet you have delicate petals; fragrant, but you have thorns that can inflict pain.
> You are in the pruning process. Some branches are being cut deeper and shorter than others, but this will enable the whole rose to grow healthier and stronger and to bloom more profusely.
> Have you not looked at a rose bush in winter? Does it not appear dead? Yet with careful pruning, fertilizing, and watering it will surely bloom again.
> Lift up your hearts. Fear not. *Keep your eyes on Me.* Watch the rose: First the buds will reappear, then you will see a rose more beautiful and fragrant than you have ever seen before.
> This rose is in My garden, and I am the Gardener (italics added).

Then again, several months later, God spoke these words of encouragement:

My Children

> Why do you fret? I have not forsaken you.
> If My voice was silenced, you were not listening quietly. I have always been here with you.
> Stand firm! The battle has begun. *Put on My full armor.* Prepare your army. Take up My sword and stand proud with My breastplate firmly against you. I will be standing beside you.
> Righteousness will prevail (italics added).

The story of this conflict is in the details of the chapters of this book. And it is perfectly framed by these prophecies. God spoke His will into our experiencing of rebellious conflict: grace in suffering through the divisiveness of others and oppressive spiritual warfare; submission in listening to the Gardener's voice; and perseverance in remaining faithful and fruitful in His garden.

Anointed prophecy also framed our vision for the future. Shortly after the "My Children" prophecy, God spoke again, calling us to be strong, trust in Him, and join Him in the great harvest:

My Children, My Gathering

> Stand strong. Lean not on your own understanding, but trust in Me. Have I not shown you how much I love you? I have brought you out of the desert. You are about to taste the sweet water of life like you have never tasted it before.

> I have heard your prayers. How many times you knocked. I have opened the door. *Step over the threshold.* The great harvest has begun, and through your obedience to Me you will witness this with your own eyes. You are My beloved. I am your Lord, your God in heaven and on earth (italics added).

God's vision for our future concerns the great harvest, not the great hibernation. This reframed our future in accordance with the Great Commission. No longer would the church's identity be confused by a group of dissenters with that of an inwardly focused gathering of people as an end in itself. Guided by the Holy Spirit and backed by Scripture, the church would continue to resist becoming a closed circle of people embracing each other—a comfortable club—caught in the illusion of safety. She would not be a gathering of people staying together in a stuck-togetherness that purchases the intactness of community at the cost of stepping over the threshold into the great harvest.[5]

The future would be stepping over the threshold both figuratively and literally—leaving behind a permanent location and joining the Great Harvest—putting the kingdom first. Community flows most naturally from missional engagement to further the kingdom, beyond our own little community. According to Alan Hirsch in *The Forgotten Ways*, "Community...'happens' to people in actual pursuit of a common vision....It involves *movement* and it describes the experience of *togetherness* that only really happens among a group of people actually engaging in a mission outside itself."[6] Anything less is pseudo-community.

Getting back to the threefold pattern: secondly, Jesus *brings us out* in order to lead us in (see Deuteronomy 6:23). He brings us out of the noise of divisiveness so that we can hear and obey

His voice as He leads us into kingdom work. Thirdly, Jesus *brings us to* Himself—not to change our circumstances but to use our circumstances for His glory. God said to Moses, "What is in your hand?" (Exodus 4:2). Jesus has already given us everything we need to live out our calling to make disciples.

When Jesus brings us to Himself, He is bringing us back full force to our first love. Perhaps you have "abandoned" or "forsaken" a fervent desire to praise and follow Jesus because of the intense, crazy conflict you have just been through. You have not lost your first love, but you have withdrawn at least to some degree from your first love.

What does it mean to withdraw from your first love? If we turn to the second chapter of Revelation, we read that the church at Ephesus is commended for diligence in duty: service to Christ. But they are charged with having forsaken their first love: love of Christ. They had lost their passion. We need to understand that the church at Ephesus did not forsake the *object* of their love but the fervent *degree* of their love of Christ. Their devotion to Christ cooled off. Perhaps yours has too, as you have suffered through an extended period of personal distress and corporate discord.

First Feelings and First Works

It might be helpful in your present circumstance to consider what love of Christ means and what it looks like. Remember that *love* is a verb. It is revealed through expression (feelings) and action (works). Love of Christ—our first love—is comprised of first feelings (what it means) and first works (what it looks like).

First feelings are all about self-denial and being vulnerable and transparent. It is total abandonment of our *self*-love and submission to the One who first loved us, gave His life for us, and is our Life: sweet Jesus. G. Campbell Morgan portrays this beautifully:

> First love is the love of espousal. Its notes are simplicity, and purity, marital love, the response of love to love, the subjection of a great love to a great love, the submission of a self-denying love to a love that denies self. First love is the abandonment of all for a love that has abandoned all.[7]

A major underpinning of the present book is the bridal dignity of the church as revealed in the doctrine of the love of espousal of Christ and the church. The manifold splendors of the marriage of Christ and His bride are captured brilliantly by Claude Chavasse in his classic book *The Bride of Christ*. He makes a forceful case and laments that for centuries there has been a growing inclination "to dismiss the doctrine as a mere metaphor."[8] Chavasse observes that theologians and Christians in general in his day (which is also true in ours) let this doctrine fade from consciousness into obscurity. Among other things, which I will not pursue here, there has been a clear shift in importance from the church in her mystical glory as the bride of Christ to a more functional emphasis on the church as the body of Christ:

> In modern theology it is common to speak almost exclusively of the Incarnation and the Church in terms of St. Paul's image of the Body, which he borrowed from the Platonic idea of the Community. But this can never replace all the fullness of the Marriage. It cannot express the fundamental and original apart-ness of Man and the Word

of God, nor the astounding love which impelled the Bridegroom to come down from heaven, to humble himself to the level of his creation, that, in uniting himself to humanity, he might raise humanity to the heaven from which he came. A Body is a unity which was always one. A Marriage is the union of two which grows into perfect unity through love.[9]

Chavasee's critique also points out that Christ's *incarnation* is represented not only by the body but also by the bride, both being "the continuation of Christ's Incarnation." Furthermore, he concludes that the fundamental biblical truth underlying "the whole elaborate doctrine of the Church as the...Body of Christ" is that "she is only the Body of Christ because she is primarily the...Bride of Christ."[10] In summary, we conclude that the church as the bride of Christ is the fundamental biblical doctrine that gives bridal dignity to the church and incarnational meaning to the church as the body of Christ.

The special place in the kingdom of the bride of Christ is especially evident in the sacraments of baptism and communion. *Baptism* symbolizes the washing away of our sins and entering into the purity of the bride. It is entering into the redemptive flow of the finished work on the cross, where "Christ loved the church and gave himself up for her to make her holy, cleansing her by the washing with water through the word, and to present her to himself as a radiant church, without stain or wrinkle or any other blemish, but holy and blameless" (Ephesians 5:25–27).

Communion symbolizes "the consummation of Christ's Marriage with his Church. What could be more beautiful than the 'Communion' of Bride with Bridegroom, of Bridegroom with Bride?"[11] It is receiving "the sweet embrace of

Communion with him who once renounced His royal state, who gave up all, who endured and overcame for the sake of...the glorified Bride of his Heart...; it is the joy of Christ as he embraces the whole Church."[12]

But as Christ embraces the whole church as His bride, His joy is "spoiled by those blemishes, those imperfections, which hinder unity and mar her beauty."[13] Therefore, every time we—together as one body and not merely as a collection of individuals—celebrate communion, we must come dressed "in fine (radiant) linen—dazzling and white, for the fine linen is (signifies, represents) the righteousness—the upright, just and godly living [deeds, conduct] and right standing with God—of the saints (God's holy people)" (Revelation 19:8, AMP). On earth, as it is in heaven!

Contrast the biblical bride of Christ—a community that embodies "purity, marital love, the response of love to love" (Morgan's words)—with what you have just gone through: an environment poisoned by distorted reality and hostility—produced by the agitating passions warring within the unsanctified self of those who chose to "fight their own demons" by leading others into the sin of rebellion. Ken Sande in his book coauthored with Tom Raabe, *Peacemaking with Families*, describes your ordeal in a slightly different but equally potent manner:

> Conflicts arise from unmet desires in our hearts. When we feel we cannot be satisfied unless we have something we want or think we need, the desire turns into a demand. If someone fails to meet that desire, we condemn him in our heart and quarrel and fight to get our way. In short, conflict arises when *desires* grow into *demands*

and we *judge* and *punish* those who get in our way (italics added).[14]

Sande has hit the nail on the head. And his analysis of the root cause of destructive conflict is totally in line with Scripture: "What causes fights and quarrels among you? Don't they come from your desires that battle within you? You want something but don't get it. You kill and covet, but you cannot have what you want. You quarrel and fight" (James 4:1–2). Inflicting pain on others is a sure sign that some selfish desire is ruling our heart. So the inner turmoil is acted out. It doesn't have to be overtly abusive. It can be more subtle and just as effective: withdrawing from relationships and activities, acting sad and gloomy, and being perpetually critical and quick to take offense. These are all common ways of hurting others, both in our families and in our churches.

Notice the huge disconnect between the simplicity, submission, and sweetness of Jesus in the Morgan quote and the demands, judgment, and punishment of leadership in the Sande quote. It should be abundantly clear how we can fall away from our first love. When we're being attacked, it's very tempting to hold onto Jesus with one hand and fight back against the rebellion with the other. It's easy to see how we can gradually and unintentionally be distracted and defensively withdraw in anger and confusion from our first love. It's hard for savagery and sweetness to coexist.

Coping with the self-willed savagery of the greed and lawlessness of unrepentant antagonists is not the only way we can drift away from our first love. Dallas Willard reminds us of another more subtle phenomenon to guard against:

> Without consciously intending to do so [we can] extinguish the...fire...[and the] operation may continue under the name, trading in memorabilia....It is never, primarily, a failure of belief or correct doctrine, or a conscious decision. It is a subtle shifting of vision, of feeling and will—of how people see things and feel about things, especially about themselves and what they are doing.[15]

Willard is suggesting that first feelings are fueled by the *fire of God*. Wherever God is, there is fire. In Scripture, God is described as a consuming fire. (See Deuteronomy 4:24 and Hebrews 12:29.) Fire is also presented as evidence of God's glory and manifest presence, as a demonstration of His holiness and power. (See Exodus 24:17 and 2 Chronicles 7:1–3.)

Fire does many things. Henry Blackaby and Ron Owens list a few in their book titled *Worship*:

> Fire gives light; fire warms; it purifies, melts, heats, cleanses, and consumes. Fire also produces power when correctly harnessed and channeled. How did God make His presence known on the Day of Pentecost? Tongues of fire descended upon the worshiping followers of Christ in the upper room. Immediately after God had manifested His glory in this way, they went forth into the world, in power, to turn their world upside down.[16]

The fire of God—the glory of God—is the fundamental organizing reality of effective ministry. Without the glory of God, ministry is fruitless. We must *sustain the fire*. We must not prevent the fire of God from being manifested by our indifference to the simplicity, tenderness, and passion of our love of Christ, or by a subtle shifting of our vision away from furthering the cause of Christ. Nor do we dare privatize the fire of God that burns within our heart. We must not keep Jesus to ourselves, either individually or corporately.

Especially in times of conflict we must be careful not to allow anyone to pervert the fire of God. I have already mentioned the subtle shifting of the vision for the church's ministry. Far more perverse is the intentional stifling of the vision by "vision vampires," who smother the fire:

- By depriving it of air—e.g. quenching the Holy Spirit by despising authentic intercessory prayer and anointed prophetic ministry and by being unwilling to submit to spiritual authority
- By putting up a smoke screen of deception—e.g. lying and secretly sowing discord and division

Returning to the proposition that love of Christ—first love—is comprised of first feelings and first works, we turn now to first works. First works *spread the fire* of God.

Bear in mind that Jesus said to the church at Ephesus, "I have this against you, that you have abandoned the love you had at first" (Revelation 2:4, RSV). Then He told them to think where they were before, repent and do the works they did at first:

- Remember—recall the simplicity and tenderness of your love of Christ and your passion for Christ.
- Repent—turn around and come back wholeheartedly to Christ.

- Return—get back to the basics of teaching, fellowship, communion, and prayer (Acts 2:42) and keep your hearts on fire for Christ.

There are other basics we could add, but of special note is the first work that Jesus Himself emphatically put at the very center of the life of the church: disciple-making. Making disciples is the primary reason for being a church and the preferred plan for spreading the fire of God. God has given us the authority and the vision to be His agents for furthering His kingdom, on earth as it is in heaven.

But let's be careful how we do this. The biblical vision of disciple-making is unequivocally stated in Matthew 28:18–20. However, if we read it in the King James Version, we pick up somewhat of an imperial tone that is consistent with colonial expansionism: "power…go…teach…world." Much missionary work in the past has used that particular wording to frame the task of spreading the gospel as a burden to be carried rather than a passion for Jesus to be shared, a program rather than the work of the Holy Spirit.

Modern translations are truer to Matthew's recollection: "authority…go…make disciples…age." Matthew emphasizes not the teaching in and of itself as much as its purpose, making disciples of Jesus who live the way He taught. And in the end, it is not just about "the ends of the earth" (as many have interpreted this passage) but the end of the age—the end of time:

> Jesus…gave his charge: "God authorized and commanded me to commission you: Go out and train everyone you meet, far and near, in this way of life, marking them by baptism in the threefold name: Father, Son, and Holy Spirit. Then instruct

> them in the practice of all I have commanded you. *I'll be with you as you do this,* day after day after day, right up to the end of the age."
> —MATTHEW 28:18–20, THE MESSAGE
> (ITALICS ADDED)

I am thankful that Jesus is with us, day after day. I am thankful that Jesus is with us throughout our conflicts, and that He will be with us and guide us in the days yet to come. I also want to give a word of blessing to those faithful disciples of Jesus in congregations that have been victimized by jealous, selfish, and arrogant instigators of rebellion. You have been made to feel discouraged, disenfranchised, and dismissed by fellow believers. I have seen as a result of my critical analysis of church conflict that there are two kinds of believers, characterized by two kinds of wisdom. Hear the Word of the Lord:

> Who is wise and understanding among you? Let him show it by his good life, by deeds done in the humility that comes from wisdom. But if you harbor bitter envy and selfish ambition in your hearts, do not boast about it or deny the truth. Such "wisdom" does not come down from heaven but is earthly, unspiritual, of the devil. For where you have envy and selfish ambition, there you find disorder and every evil practice.
>
> But the wisdom that comes from heaven is first of all pure; then peace-loving, considerate, submissive, full of mercy and good fruit, impartial and sincere. Peacemakers who sow in peace raise a harvest of righteousness.
> —JAMES 3:13–18

Reflecting on Loose Ends

WHAT IF? WHAT if I had done this? What if I had done that? What if I had done something else? What if I had not done such and such? The what ifs are endless. And they're relentless. And they'll suffocate you. They'll take the life right out of you.

What ifs are not from the Holy Spirit. He does not take the life out of you. Jesus is your Life. There is none other. If the question is, What if? the answer is, in the words of the great old hymn, "Hallelujah, what a Savior!"

However, after we have recovered from the confusion/conflict (as discussed in Chapter 7), we still have recurring negative thoughts and unsettling emotions. They come and go, not worthy of further examination. It's Satan tempting us with a prick here and a prod there. Come on, get mad again. Feel that helplessness again. Remember those lost opportunities. How could you have been so stupid? That's Satan talking. It is not revelation from God. Quite the opposite. It is the recurrence of evil.

The Problem of Evil

We must remember that evil is absolutely the most serious problem that could occur in any conflict. Satan will use conflict every chance he gets. This does not mean that every conflict is evil. It does mean that there is no more fertile ground for satanic activity. Conflict brings with it an untold number of openings for Satan to establish footholds in people to distort the conflict for his own diabolical purposes. What more effective way could he possibly use to bring down a strong, healthy church?

Think back to your recent conflict with brothers and sisters in Christ. I assume you loved them, forgave them, and still love them. You are living at peace with them, but at a distance, even though you know they are not and never were the enemy. The real enemy is Satan. He got in through some open doors in their lives that may or may not have been known to you, and through them contaminated the entire church. Is there any other possible way to explain their outrageous behavior?

Do you remember having uneasy, queasy feelings during the conflict when you were around them? How your heart may have embraced them, but your hands could not touch them? How you may have "felt" evil in their presence and perhaps even "saw" evil manifested in their being? (For example, I was in a rebellious conflict situation where a person with the gift of discernment of spirits saw a cobra head on one of the fiercest agitators.)

Do you remember that it was difficult to get the agitators to talk with you directly or honestly? Did they refuse to accept your requests to talk with them about their concerns? Or, did you have to go on a "fishing expedition" with them, seeking to clarify your suspicions only to be met with defensive accusations and denial? Did their belligerent behavior make it inadvisable for you to pursue them with your concerns? It's tough to deal with evil, isn't it?

The problem is not just the effects of evil but evil itself. Unfortunately, we have a chronic inability in the church to recognize evil and respond to it effectively. Consider that when we attribute wicked behavior to demonic influence, some people will automatically counter that sinful nature must have been the cause. Could that be because labeling it sin intuitively makes it more manageable and easier to confine? Others wrongly conclude that so-called evil behavior is a developmental problem that causes bad behavior, which must be treated rather like a disease! Approaches like these marginalize evil, which is at its worst in postmodernism with its false claims that all judgments of evil are evil themselves. Taking evil per se out of the equation is a philosophical commitment to moral equivalence and the additional false claim that all sins are equal (debunking the latter claim has been independently corroborated by others[1]).

The fatal flaw in dealing with conflict is the marginalizing of evil. That can be an unintended outcome in striving to find the good that can come out of evil. God meant it for good. Too often that is taken to mean that something good or some good thing will come out of it. I prefer to say that some One will go through it with me. My hope is placed in the companionship of Jesus through the suffering, not in the compensation of something good for having gone through the suffering. Os Guinness in his book *Unspeakable* cautions us: "There is usually at least some positive side to evil and suffering, and it is healthy to recognize it—though finding the good in evil and suffering must never be misused as an explanation for why the evil occurred in the first place."[2]

Guinness also warns against the flawed thinking that evil is simply the result of wicked monsters, thereby making it rare and a thing of the past. He especially warns against denying that evil is an objective reality: "The only evil left, in this view, is the fact that human beings suffer. Put simply, evil was once the source of suffering, but for many people today, suffering…is the only source of evil."[3]

The marginalizing of evil can be seen throughout our

postmodern culture, specifically in ways that prepare the soil for demonic activity in church conflict. Guinness identifies one such cultural influence: "At the heart of the modern world is a refusal to accept any limits and therefore a drive to cross lines, to break taboos...to celebrate a culture of transgression."[4] Guinness got it exactly right. We have allowed the *culture of transgression* to seep into the church, in the host of ways depicted throughout this book. The societal breakdown of courtesy, consideration for others, and civility has led to a general disregard for common social graces. They're not common anymore!

The culture of transgression can easily enter the church via patterns of behavior learned in members' families. For example, I have personally witnessed a very angry man standing up during a worship service, and thrusting a pointed finger and shouting at the pastor, "You'd better repent!"[5] It was a barbaric, shocking display of disrespect for pastoral authority and defilement of the gathering of God's people for worship. Afterward, some people in the congregation physically shook and cried, and later in the day some got headaches and vomited. At another congregational meeting, the man's angry teenage son stood and pointed and shouted slanderous accusations at the pastor. Like father, like son: blatant disrespect for the spiritual authority of the pastor and for the pastor as a person.

We dare not permit the marginalizing of evil, especially in the case of the Lord's warning in His response to rebellion. In Isaiah 50:11 (BERKELEY) we read: "Look, all you who kindle the fire and set off the sparks—walk in the light you have lit. This comes to you from My hand; you shall lie down in torment." Those who kindle the fire and set off the sparks of rebellious sin must walk in their own light—not the Lord's—and thereby suffer torment of their own making. Marginalizing evil is wrong in the sight of the Lord. Therefore, we absolutely must promote the centrality of evil as a possibility in the explanation of any given conflict in the church. Guinness puts it in the perspective of the examined life:

> For a reflective person, life must be examined, and it is almost certain to be tested. Evil is neither one test among others nor one mystery among others. It is the supreme test and the profoundest mystery in light of which all other tests and mysteries will be judged.[6]

THE PROBLEM WITH CONSEQUENCES

When people kindle the fire of evil, they have to walk in the light of it, and suffer torment of their own making. When they do not repent and it happens to them, it creates a real problem for me: How should I respond? What is the appropriate response when unrepentant troublemakers begin to suffer the consequences of their actions?

I struggle with the natural human tendency to take some degree of satisfaction in seeing people experience pain and loss—as Scripture says they will—because of their grievous sin toward other Christians in the congregation. When they profane the name of the Lord and defile the gathering together of His people, or when they follow false "teachers" and "prophets" and complain that they are not getting what they want, and God gives it to them (see Numbers 11!), they will suffer consequences for their sin.

I believe that it is right to rejoice when the Lord demonstrates His righteousness in those situations. But not only must my rejoicing be confined to the Lord and His righteousness, it must also be tempered with sorrow. I am deeply saddened by the inevitable pain and suffering of those who are the primary conduits of spiritual warfare, who know not what they do. They may be actively participating in the evil enterprise of attacking the bride of Christ or have ceased doing so and have not repented. But they are still my brothers and sisters in Christ. I love them and forgive them, and I shudder when I think about what they will go through or are presently going through for what they are doing or have done.

I firmly believe that while I continue to personally mourn the loss of covenantal relationship with friends and coworkers in the cause of Christ, I will find *final peace* only with the restoration of righteousness, which must precede the genuine reconciliation of those relationships. As a reminder, these are the biblical steps to make that happen:

1. Recognition of God's utter disdain for those who intentionally cause division.//
2. Unconditional forgiveness of the leaders of rebellion—the primary conduits of spiritual warfare.
3. Repentance by the leaders of rebellion.
4. Restoration of righteousness—the purity of the bride of Christ.
5. Genuine reconciliation of righteous relationships. It is never too late.

Psalm 7 (we can place the original setting of this psalm in Absalom's rebellion against David) speaks to both unrepented rebellion and unrestored righteousness, in verses 11 through 17:

> God is a righteous judge.
>
> If a man does not repent, God will sharpen his sword.
>
> He who is pregnant with evil and conceives trouble gives birth to disillusionment [lies].
>
> He who digs a hole and scoops it out falls into the pit he has made.
>
> The trouble he causes recoils on himself; his violence comes down on his own head.
>
> I will give thanks to the Lord because of his righteousness and will sing praise to the name of the Lord Most High.

What is the appropriate response when unrepentant troublemakers suffer the consequences of their sinful actions? And what am I to do while I pray for them both to be blessed and to repent? *Give thanks to the Lord because of His righteousness and sing praises to the Lord Most High.* I know that He hears both my prayers and that He will do what only He can do in response. He alone is God, and I am not. My response is to rejoice in the Lord because of who He is, regardless of the situation. To God be the glory.

The Problem with Legacies

At the end of the day, how do you want to be remembered? That's probably the question you've been asking yourself all through the conflict. It's the legacy question. It's driven by concern for your reputation and—quite possibly—by your desire to be popular, which is much more short-lived and also dangerous. An all-consuming desire for popularity can easily lead to self-deception. You begin thinking you are incomparable, indispensable, and even invincible! The legacy question is all about what difference you've made and how long it will last. It's all about your identity. And it's the wrong question.

The problem with legacies is they're all about "me." Personal identity. You may recall that in chapter 7, the point was made that it is in Jesus alone we find our identity—therefore our calling is to follow Jesus the Way, the Truth, and the Life. That is our goal and our glory. God's goal for us is not being successful but being Christlike, so that others will see His love manifested through the conflict. Paul writes in Philippians 3:14 that basically we are to press on toward the goal to win the prize, which belongs to those who respond wholeheartedly to God's call, away from self and toward complete fulfillment of life in Christ. Regarding our glory, in Colossians 1:27, Paul is crystal clear: "Christ in you, the hope of glory."

Os Guinness is very helpful with his comments about concerns regarding our "legacy," in his book titled *Prophetic Untimeliness*:

> When all that we are, and have, and do becomes a response to God's call, we live—in Oswald Chambers's famous words—"our utmost for His highest."...
>
> A simple consequence follows. If we define all that we are before our great Caller and live our lives before one audience—the Audience of One—then we cannot define or decide our own achievements and our own success. It is not for us to say what we have accomplished. It is not for us

to pronounce ourselves successful. It is not for us to spell out what our legacy has been. Indeed, it is not even for us to know. Only the Caller can say. Only the Last Day will tell. Only the final "Well done" will show what we have really done.[7]

It is not for us to pronounce ourselves successful. That's for the "Audience of One" to do. It is not for us to proclaim, "Well done." Scripture tells us what is for us to do: "Count it all joy, my brethren, when you meet various trials, for you know that the testing of your faith produces steadfastness. And let steadfastness have its full effect, that you may be perfect and complete, lacking in nothing" (James 1:2–4, RSV).

Embrace the reality that "the testing of your faith produces steadfastness." Or as Philip Yancey says in *Disappointment with God*, trust "in advance what will only make sense in reverse."[8]

Now is the time to embrace steadfastness through the lived reality of your faith. Live your faith just like David did. Here he is addressing his Audience of One (I love his confident assertion, "as you know, O LORD"): "I proclaim righteousness in the great assembly; I do not seal my lips, as you know, O Lord. I do not hide your righteousness in my heart; I speak of your faithfulness and salvation. I do not conceal your love and your truth from the great assembly" (Psalm 40:9–10). That is the choice that must always be made. Now is the time to tie up loose ends. Give it all to Jesus so that you can be holy and whole, and as Eugene Peterson puts it in *The Message*, "not deficient in any way."

A final word for the leaders and members of the congregation:

We beg of you, brothers, to recognize the workers among you, both your leaders in the Lord and your advisers. Because of their work, hold them lovingly in the highest regard. Enjoy peace among yourselves.

But we appeal to you, brothers: warn the disorderly; cheer up the fainthearted; give your support to the weak; exercise patience toward everyone. See to it that no one pays back evil for evil....

Always be cheerful. Pray unceasingly. Under all circumstances give thanks, for such is God's will for you in Christ Jesus.

—1 Thessalonians 5:12-18, Berkeley

And may the Lord of peace Himself grant you peace at all times under all circumstances. The Lord be with you all.

—2 Thessalonians 3:16, Berkeley

Appendix

Acknowledging Transference

Sheep who are heavily involved in unhealthy church conflict owe it to themselves and their church to look in the mirror at the wolves' clothing they wear to church. The following questions may be helpful:

- Are my thoughts preoccupied with a specific person or situation, so much so that I lose sleep thinking about him or her?
- Do I frequently hold imaginary conversations in my head with this person?
- Do I often find myself telling others about my relationship with this person, whether praising him or her idealistically or venting criticism?
- When I think of this person, do I frequently struggle with envy or jealousy?
- Do I often wonder about what he or she is thinking or feeling about me?
- Am I judging him or her as I read Scripture?
- Have I first idealized and then despised this person?

- Do I lavishly flatter this person on occasion and then turn around later and publicly engage in outbursts of tantrum-like anger, physically or verbally against him or her?

- Do I often overreact to small offenses from this person?

- Have I imagined wrongs that were not there or blown out of proportion those that were unintentional?[1]

If some of these questions apply to you, you may be inappropriately using your relationship with this individual to manage personal unresolved problems that you are not dealing with in some other relationship. If so, you must repent of the sins of your transference and ask for forgiveness.

Appendix

Acknowledging Self-Deception

If you suspect you may have believed something based on merely suggestive evidence, are you ready to faithfully check out the actual facts? Are you also willing to check out other ways that you may have been deceiving yourself? The following questions may be helpful:

- Do I disguise my unresolved anger as "concern" for someone, or feeling "sad" for him or her, to justify my bahavior toward that person?

- Have I believed that I have forgiven someone and that I am no longer angry at him or her but have not been able to refrain from constant criticism and vindictiveness toward that person?

- Do I find myself treating others with lack of moral sensitivity and respect?

- Have I intentionally managed my own beliefs by manipulating someone else's beliefs, without regard for the truth?

- Do I believe something is true because I know the Bible actually says so, or must I admit that the real source of my conviction is that I just "know for sure in my gut"?

- Do I discredit matters of the mind and give nearly exclusive emphasis to "the heart"?
- Have I joined a group of people who have the illusion of invulnerability?
- Do I find that the group's illusion of unity keeps me from expressing doubts and concerns about the group's beliefs?
- Does this group believe in the inherent morality or rightness of their cause, and therefore they do not take responsibility for their mistreatment of others?
- Does this group disrespect spiritual authority and discount biblical warnings about the consequences of their actions?[1]

If you are living a lie, you must separate yourself from any group that reinforces your self-deception. And you must be intentional about progressively finding your way back to the truth.

NOTES

INTRODUCTION

1. Warren Bennis, *Why Leaders Can't Lead: The Unconscious Conspiracy Continues* (San Francisco: Jossey-Bass, 1989), 148.

2. See *Wounded Workers: Recovering from Heartache in the Workplace and the Church*, by Kirk E. Farnsworth (Mukilteo, WA: WinePress, 1998).

3. These two books serve as bookends for a trilogy—unhealthy churches and wounded people, healthy churches and healthy people, and unhealthy people and wounded churches. See also *All Churches Great and Small: 60 Ideas for Improving Your Church's Ministry*, by Kirk and Rosie Farnsworth (Valley Forge, PA: Judson, 2005).

4. This is an application of the widely acclaimed insights in *Experiencing God: How to Live the Full Adventure of Knowing and Doing the Will of God*, by Henry T. Blackaby and Claude V. King (Nashville: Broadman & Holman, 1994).

5. Chris Jackson, "She Loves Me, She Loves Me Not: Responding to Criticism in the Church," *Ministry Today*, January/February 2009, 34.

1—REVIEWING UNDERLYING ISSUES

1. "Statistics About Pastors," Maranatha Life's *Life-Line for Pastors* (cited June 18, 2008). Online: http://www.maranathalife.com/lifeline/stats.htm.

2. Eric Reed, "Leadership Surveys Church Conflict," *Leadership Journal*, fall 2004.

3. See *The Disciple-Making Pastor: Leading Others on the Journey of Faith*, by Bill Hull (Grand Rapids, MI: Baker, 2007).

4. Ibid., 111–112.

5. Ibid., 50.

6. Ibid., 65.

7. Ibid., 223–224.

8. Ibid., 46.

9. See *Reveal: Where Are You?* by Greg L. Hawkins, Cally Parkinson and Eric Arnson (Barrington, IL: Willow, 2007).

10. Ibid., 41.

11. Ibid., 47.

12. Tom White, *Breaking Strongholds: How Spiritual Warfare Sets Captives Free* (Ann Arbor, MI: Servant, 1993), 40.

13. Taken with modification from White, *Breaking Strongholds*, 50.

14. Inspired by White, *Breaking Strongholds*, 124.

2—Revealing Psychological Dynamics

1. These are the four reasons that warrant removing a pastor, according to the *Didache*, written in the early second century, the oldest known Christian treatise on the organization of the local church.

2. It should be noted that although the pastor's own family system, as well as the systemic features of the church organization, can also contribute to the overall dynamic of the conflict, they are not the main focus of this book.

3. Edwin H. Friedman, *Generation to Generation: Family Process in Church and Synagogue* (New York: Guilford, 1985), 26.

4. Ibid., 198.

5. Ibid., 208.

6. Ibid., 50.

7. Valerie J. McIntyre, *Sheep in Wolves' Clothing: How Unseen Need Destroys Friendship and Community and What to Do about It* (Grand Rapids, MI: Baker, 1999), 84.

8. Ibid., 84–85.

9. Ibid., 92–93.

10. Ibid., 92–94.

11. Ibid., 92, 94–95.

12. Gregg A. Ten Elshof, *I told Me So: Self-Deception and the Christian Life* (Grand Rapids, MI: William B. Eerdmans, 2009).

13. Ibid., 76.

14. Ibid., 88.

15. Ibid., 93.

16. Ibid., 117.

3—Recognizing Spiritual Warfare

1. Francis Frangipane, *A House United: How Christ-Centered Unity Can End Church Division* (Grand Rapids, MI: Chosen, 2005), 15–16, 21–23.

2. Francis Frangipane, *The Three Battlegrounds: An In-Depth View of the Three Arenas of Spiritual Warfare: The Mind, the Church and the Heavenly Places* (Cedar Rapids, IA: Arrow, 1989), 37.

3. E. Stanley Jones, *A Song of Ascents: A Spiritual Autobiography* (Nashville: Abingdon, 1968), 52–53. According to Jones, the unconverted subconscious is that unsurrendered, unredeemed part of the self that can play a major role in the actions of believers who cause division in the church. He concludes in *Victory through Surrender* (Nashville: Abingdon, 1966), 92-93:

> Actions are usually determined by the will, but…reactions come out of the subconscious, and the subconscious is where the unsurrendered self lurks. Touch it and it will

blow its top. The modes of life come out of the conscious, but the moods of life come out of the subconscious. So the conversion of the actions is important, but the conversion of the reactions is just as important or in some ways more important than the actions. Without a complete self-surrender the conversion of the reactions is impossible.

4. Frangipane, *The Three Battlegrounds*, 21.

5. See this progression perceptively detailed in *The Divine Conspiracy: Rediscovering Our Hidden Life in God*, by Dallas Willard (New York: HarperSanFrancisco, 1998).

6. Ibid., 149.

7. Frangipane, *The Three Battlegrounds*, 77.

8. Merrill F. Unger, *What Demons Can Do to Saints* (Chicago: Moody, 1991), 61.

9. Kenneth C. Haugk, *Antagonists in the Church: How to Identify and Deal with Destructive Conflict* (Minneapolis: Augsburg, 1988), 25–26.

10. I have selected a few of the ideas, with some modification consistent with the author's intent.

11. Haugk, *Antagonists in the Church*, 27.

12. See *The Wounded Minister: Healing from and Preventing Personal Attacks*, by Guy Greenfield (Grand Rapids, MI: Baker, 2001); Haugk, *Antagonists in the Church*; *Clergy Killers: Guidance for Pastors and Congregations Under Attack*, by G. Lloyd Rediger (Louisville, KY: Westminster John Knox, 1997).

13. Frangipane, *A House United*, 128.

14. Frangipane, *The Three Battlegrounds*, 92.

15. I am indebted to Frangipane, *The Three Battlegrounds* (see pp. 86, 132), and Richard W. Greene, "God's Manifold Wisdom," presented at Keystone Project, Keystone, SD, April 2008, for developing this line of thought regarding the battleground in the heavenlies. Keystone Project is a global network of churches and leaders committed to launching disciple-making movements throughout the world for the fulfillment of the Great Commission in this generation and beyond.

16. Fuchsia Pickett, *The Next Move of God* (Orlando, FL: Creation House, 1994), 59.

17. Frangipane, *The Three Battlegrounds*, 98.

18. Ibid., 104.

19. Pickett, *The Next Move of God*, 45.

20. Taken with additions and modifications from John Paul Jackson, *Unmasking the Jezebel Spirit* (North Sutton, NH: Streams, 2002), 169–172.

4—Restoring Church Purity

1. This is a condensed amalgamation with slight modification of Proverbs 6:12–19 (AMP, NIV).

2. Charles F. Pfeiffer and Everett F. Harrison, eds., *The Wycliffe Bible Commentary* (Chicago: Moody, 1962), 563.

3. Jackson, *Unmasking the Jezebel Spirit*, 80.

4. Ken Sande, *The Peacemaker: A Biblical Guide to Resolving Personal Conflict*, 3rd ed. (Grand Rapids, MI: Baker, 2004), 124.

5. Ibid.

6. Ibid.

7. Frangipane, *A House United*, 103.

8. Ibid., 44–45.

9. Ibid., 49.

10. Ibid., 46.

11. Jackson, *Unmasking the Jezebel Spirit*, 81.

12. Ibid., 82.

13. Inspired by terminology used by Friedman, *Generation to Generation*, 228.

14. Farnsworth, *Wounded Workers*, 172–176.

15. See Jim Van Yperen, *Making Peace: A Guide to Overcoming Church Conflict* (Chicago: Moody, 2002).

16. See *Church Discipline That Heals: Putting Costly Love into Action*, by John White and Ken Blue (Downers Grove, IL: InterVarsity, 1985).

17. Ibid., 20.

18. Ibid., 59.

19. Ibid., 69-70.

20. G. Campbell Morgan, *A First Century Message to Twentieth Century Christians* (New York: Fleming H. Revell, 1902), 107. This is a paraphrase of James 3:17.

5—Resolving the Conflict

1. See Haugk, *Antagonists in the Church*, 48–51. Haugk weighs in on the issue of universal application of Matthew 18 regardless of the type of conflict (healthy or unhealthy): automatic use of the first three steps in every case. First, he cautions us to be aware of the manipulative power of pathological antagonists (see Chapter 3).

> Antagonists are all too adept at turning the tables, and there are many instances where a formal first-stage Matthew admonition was used by an antagonist as an occasion to assail the one beginning the process. This was

further compounded when the injured party returned with two others, as directed by step two of the process, and the antagonist proceeded to make an alliance with them against the first individual.

Second, he cautions us to use the Matthew 18 procedures as they were intended. They are disciplinary procedures for publicly known offenses, not fact-finding or negotiation procedures. Because of the insatiable, insidious belligerence of the antagonists, we must not expose ourselves and the congregation to further harm. We must stay away from them as best we can—which brings us to the tension between engagement (Matthew 18) and disengagement (for example: 1 Timothy 6; 2 Timothy 3; Romans 16; 2 Thessalonians 3; and 1 Corinthians 5). Haugk calls our attention to Titus 3:10–11 and the admonition "have nothing to do with him," referring to someone who persists in divisiveness and is not about to change. This sets up the remaining (fourth) step in Matthew 18, termination of membership, as the only constructive option. Haugk concludes:

> Titus was not to engage in extensive attempts to smooth things over with the troublemaker; he was simply to avoid that person.
>
> The apostolic guideline is clear: when confronted with an antagonist, face the *probability* that change simply will not occur. He or she is "self-condemned," in Paul's words. Stay away from that person as best you can—emotionally and physically.

2. White and Blue, *Church Discipline That Heals*, 67.
3. Ibid., 66.
4. Ibid., 59.
5. Ibid., 96.
6. Oswald Chambers, *My Utmost for His Highest*, updated ed., ed. James Reimann (Grand Rapids, MI: Discovery House, 1992), 3/31.
7. R. T. Kendall, *Total Forgiveness* (Lake Mary, FL: Charisma House, 2002), 82.
8. See Van Yperen, *Making Peace*.
9. John Howard Yoder, "Binding and Loosing" (Concern: A Pamphlet Series for Questions of Christian Renewal, no. 14, 1967). Quoted in White and Blue, *Church Discipline That Heals*, 230–231.
10. This rather lengthy fourth observation complements and confirms from personal experience some of the comprehensive insights and findings of Kjos Ministries. Online: http://www.crossroad.to/.

11. Taken with modification from David Zarefsky, *Argumentation: The Study of Effective Reasoning*, 2nd ed. (Chantilly, VA: The Teaching Company, 2005), 59–60.

6—Recovering from Conflict

1. Taken with modification from Rediger, *Clergy Killers*, 9–10.
2. Henri J. M. Nouwen, *With Open Hands* (New York: Ballantine, 1972), 4–5.
3. Henri J. M. Nouwen, *The Way of the Heart* (New York: Ballantine, 1981), 15.
4. Frangipane, *The Three Battlegrounds*, 37, 7, 12, 8, 39–40, 61.
5. G. D. Watson, *Soul Food* (Cincinnati: M. W. Knapp, 1896), 81–83.
6. Cornelius Plantinga, Jr., "Rehearsing Forgiveness," *Christianity Today*, 29 April 1996, 32.
7. White and Blue, *Church Discipline That Heals*, 190.
8. Greenfield, *The Wounded Minister*, 63.
9. Ibid., 32.
10. Ibid., 60.

7—Reframing the Future

1. This is a condensed amalgamation with slight modification of Psalm 93 (AMP, NIV).
2. This discussion of finishing well was inspired and guided by the brilliant presentation of Jesus' way in *The Jesus Way: A Conversation on the Ways That Jesus Is the Way*, by Eugene H. Peterson (Grand Rapids, MI: William B. Eerdmans, 2007).
3. Dallas Willard, *The Great Omission: Reclaiming Jesus's Essential Teachings on Discipleship* (New York: HarperSanFrancisco, 2006), 99.
4. Ibid., 101.
5. See Acts 10:47; 11:15–18; Romans 8:9; 1 Corinthians 12:13; and Galatians 3:1–14.
6. I am indebted to Richard W. Greene, "Identity *before* Community," Keystone Project, April 2008, for this discussion of Jesus the Life.
7. Inspired by Richard W. Greene, Keystone Project, April 2008.
8. Taken from Richard W. Greene, "The Seven Core Values," Keystone Project, April 2008.
9. Taken with modification from Hull, *The Disciple-Making Pastor*, 13.
10. I am indebted to Richard W. Greene, "Sarah and Hagar," Keystone Project, April 2008, for this discussion of Galatians 4:21–31.

8—Returning to Your First Love

1. Finding peace is a process, similar to finishing well, of redeeming conflict by bringing it under the lordship of Jesus Christ (see Chapter 7). I differentiate among keeping peace, making peace, and finding peace—or fleeing conflict, fighting conflict, and *freeing* conflict. Keeping peace is more about resisting conflict, making peace more about resolving conflict, and finding peace more about *redeeming* conflict—restraining (controlling, repressing), repairing (rebuilding, reorganizing) and *refining* (cleansing, purifying). In a word, responding to conflict is not about flight or fight. It's about follow. And it's about purity: "The fruit of righteousness will be peace" (Isaiah 32:17).

2. Melchizedek in the Old Testament (Genesis 14:18–20; Psalm 110:4) as a type of Christ is symbolic of the connection between righteousness and peace. In the New Testament we read, "This Melchizedek was king of Salem and priest of God Most High.... First, his name means 'king of righteousness'; then also, 'king of Salem' means 'king of peace'" (Hebrews 7:1–2). I like the way the King James Version makes it a bit more emphatic: "...and after that also..." (v. 2). In other words, righteousness first, and after that, peace.

3. Jack Deere, *The Beginner's Guide to the Gift of Prophecy* (Ventura, CA: Regal, 2001), 37.

4. Fuchsia Pickett, *Presenting the Holy Spirit* (Lake Mary, FL: Creation House, 1997), 109.

5. Inspired by terminology used by Friedman, *Generation to Generation*, 228.

6. Alan Hirsch, *The Forgotten Ways: Reactivating the Missional Church* (Grand Rapids, MI: Brazos, forthcoming). Quoted in Michael Frost, *Exiles: Living Missionally in a Post-Christian Culture* (Peabody, MA: Hendrickson, 2006), 123.

7. Morgan, *A First Century Message to Twentieth Century Christians*, 42.

8. Claude Chavasse, *The Bride of Christ: An Enquiry into the Nuptial Element in Early Christianity* (London: The Religious Book Club, 1939), 162.

9. Ibid., 16–17.

10. Ibid., 70–71.

11. Ibid., 108.

12. Ibid., 227.

13. Ibid.

14. Ken Sande and Tom Raabe, *Peacemaking for Families: A Biblical Guide to Managing Conflict in Your Home* (Wheaton, IL: Tyndale, 2002), 16. See also "Getting to the Heart of Conflict" at www.Peacemaker.net.

15. Willard, *The Great Omission*, 93.

16. Henry Blackaby and Ron Owens, *Worship: Believers Experiencing God* (Nashville: LifeWay, 2001), 92.

9—Reflecting on Loose Ends

1. For example, Cornelius Plantinga, Jr. unequivocally states in *Not the Way It's Supposed to Be: A Breviary of Sin* (Grand Rapids, MI: William B. Eerdmans, 1995), 21–22:

> All sin is equally wrong, but not all sin is equally bad. Acts are either right or wrong, either consonant with God's will or not. But among good acts some are better than others, and among wrong acts some worse than others.…This distinction is standard in much of the Christian tradition, Protestant as well as Catholic. Consider the Second Helvetic Confession, chap. 8: "We…confess that sins are not equal…some are more serious than others."…
>
> The badness or seriousness of sin depends to some degree on the amount and kind of damage it inflicts…and to some degree on the personal investment and motive of the sinner.…[Therefore involuntary sin] is a less serious offense than [voluntary sin].

2. Os Guinness, *Unspeakable: Facing Up to Evil in an Age of Genocide and Terror* (New York: HarperSanFrancisco, 2005), 12–13.

3. Ibid., 24.

4. Ibid., 103.

5. This is reminiscent of the scriptural account of Jesus casting out an evil spirit, which begins with a man who was possessed by an evil spirit shouting in the synagogue at Jesus. Interestingly the demonic manifestation occurred in both the situation I was in and Jesus' situation in reaction to authoritative teaching. (See Mark 1:23–24.)

6. Guinness, *Unspeakable*, 238.

7. Os Guinness, *Prophetic Untimeliness: A Challenge to the Idol of Relevance* (Grand Rapids, MI: Baker, 2003), 92–93.

8. Philip Yancey, *Disappointment with God: Three Questions No One Asks Aloud* (Grand Rapids, MI: Zondervan, 1988), 224. This insightful, inspired book is especially helpful in bringing the darkness of disappointment in the apparent unfairness of God into the light of the awesome faithfulness of God. This quote is from Yancey's brilliant analysis of the Book of Job—the oldest book in the Bible and the Bible's most complete treatment of the puzzle of human suffering.

Appendix I:
Acknowledging Transference

1. Taken with additions and modifications from McIntyre, *Sheep in Wolves' Clothing*, 137–138.

Appendix II:
Acknowledging Self-Deception

1. Taken with additions and modifications from Ten Elshof, *I Told Me So*, 27, 59, 70, 72–73, 87–88.

About the Author

Kirk E. Farnsworth, Ph.D., has had extensive, multi-discipline career experience as a naval officer (stationed in Japan), corporate executive (CRISTA Ministries), college professor (University of New Hampshire, Trinity College, and Wheaton College), and counseling psychologist and co-pastor of a disciple-making church with Rosie, his wife of nearly fifty years.

He is an award-winning author of six books, two of which are complementary volumes to this book, about wounded churches: *Wounded Workers* (translated into Chinese), about wounded workers in the workplace and the church and *All Churches Great and Small* (translated into Russian), about healthy churches.

Dr. Kirk and Rev. Rosie are retired and reside on agriforestry acreage near Seattle, Washington.

www.ingramcontent.com/pod-product-compliance
Lightning Source LLC
LaVergne TN
LVHW051057080426
835508LV00019B/1934